RACHEL BRUNO

Fractured Hope

A Mother's Fight for Justice

First edition

ISBN: 978-0-578-37477-2

Advisor: Mimika Cooney
Editing by Barbara Kois
Proofreading by Kathy Haskins
Illustration by Nevena Stankovic

This book was professionally typeset on Reedsy.
Find out more at reedsy.com

Contents

Invitation

As a thank you for purchasing this book I would love to gift you with the digital version of the accompanying Devotional.

Visit https://www.rachelbruno.com/fracturedhope to claim your free gift.

Acknowledgments

Dedicated to all who have ever suffered. God is the final judge.

First and foremost, my mom who taught me everything I know. This book would not have come to fruition had it not been for your example in my life. I should have listened to you in third grade, and you told me I should be a writer.

To my husband, Ricardo. God put us on a "fast track" and there's no one I would rather be on this roller coaster with than you. Thank you for being there through all the ups and downs.

To my family members in Brazil, I can't begin to express my thanks to you. The sacrifices you made putting your lives on hold to help mine.

To all my friends, in America and beyond, I am truly blessed to have had so many offer me a helping hand, a shoulder to cry on, words of encouragement, character letters, and prayers. Your support was invaluable to me.

I am extremely grateful for my legal team. This story could have turned out very differently were it not for you.

Finally, I would like to thank the editors, proofreaders, advisors, and mentors I had when writing this book. It's a jungle out there, and I couldn't have done it without your help.

Preface

Here I was at the hospital, praying over my seven-week-old son, who had just undergone brain surgery. The doctor had told me they didn't know whether he'd survive the next forty-eight hours. A thought repeatedly rang in my head as I remembered the miscarriage I had with our first baby: Not again … please … not again.

But during that thought cycle, hope crashed into my thoughts, and I hit the brakes. I said, "God, I asked for him, and You gave him to me—"

I did give him to you; he's Mine.

My thought of *not again* switched to *he's mine.* "You're right, Lord. He is Yours."

I gave him to you. Nobody is going to take him away from you. He's Mine.

Hope was reborn at that moment, at the lowest of my lows … as of yet. My heart was lifted. My strength was renewed. My burden was lessened. I breathed a sigh of relief as I surrendered my son's life to God.

My life had included a series of losses from very early in my existence, starting with my dad's passing when I was only nine months old. Five years after his death, I lost my aunt (his sister) and my grandpa (my mother's dad) in the same year. My mom and I were always on the move between the United States and Brazil. It seemed every time we were settling somewhere, something would happen, and we'd move again. I learned not to get too attached to anything, for everything could change at a moment's notice.

I opened my Bible to the verse I had chosen as a possible guide to this book: Romans 12:12, "Rejoice in hope, be patient in tribulation, be constant in prayer."

Hope. Patience. Prayer. That's how the battle against the legal and bureaucratic parties involved was won, but the war was a spiritual one.

Had I had all the money in the world, all the knowledge in the world, but had not the Word of God, I would have lost my soul and my will to live at some point.

Let's start with hope. The thought of losing my baby son Lucas at the hospital was heart-wrenching. I asked God, "Why?" But almost instantaneously, I took that back and pleaded instead, "Please, no, God ... not again, not another heartbreaking loss of someone I love."

Surrendering is an interesting phenomenon. For our entire lives, we are told to "never give up." How is surrendering any different from giving up? Surrendering gives you freedom from something you know you ultimately cannot control. You are giving it up—to the One who *is* in control. But I couldn't surrender if I didn't have my faith and eternal hope in Jesus.

Everything in this world is temporary, but God's truth remains forever. Surrender is reflected in the words: "Thy will be done." Easy to say, not so easy to live. Throughout this entire journey, I had to surrender more times than I could count, but none of it was possible without hope.

Patience. Boy, oh, boy ... the bane of my human existence. I've always said, "Don't ask God for patience 'cause He'll test you to no end." But this time was different. I wasn't dealing with the usual patience triggers like sitting in traffic forever, or repeating the same thing over and over to your spouse, who never seems to listen. My test of patience was ultimately about trust. Could I trust God through what would be some of the most nerve-wracking times in my life? Could I wait on God?

Waiting is the worst. Why? Because we feel a loss of control. We don't know what or when something is going to happen. It's all up in the air. The word *surrender* comes up again. I had to *surrender* my sense of timing, my sense of well-being, to dependence on God.

I didn't know anything but the fact that God knew all things.

And what did I do when I felt I knew nothing? *I prayed.* I learned to pray like never before during this (literal) trial. On my knees, through tears, spoken aloud, through song, through groans, in the spirit. Looking back, it's hard to describe what I was feeling and how I was dealing with everything. It was almost an out-of-body experience. My brain knew I should be panicking, should be hysterical, should be going crazy. Yet my spirit was light as a feather. It reminds me of the song "It Is Well with My Soul."

Praying brought me closer to God, who filled my soul with living water from the eternal well. Everything around me was falling apart, but it was well with my soul. Being constantly in prayer became a way of living. Before this, whenever I pictured prayer, it was always in a ritualistic, quiet, eyes closed, intercessory type of setting. Of course, there is—and should be—a time and place for that kind of prayer. But being *constant* in prayer meant living it in the Spirit. My soul was so attuned to what God was saying to me at every minute of the day that even in my tears, during my court-ordered "services" and my visitation with my sons, I was always talking to God, which kept me sane during this process.

Little droplets of biblical wisdom were always falling on the roof of my heart.

So now that I've gone through the three parts of survival—hope, patience, and prayer, I will start from the beginning.

Rachel Bruno

Nashville, Tennessee

I

Part One

1

Strength to the Powerless

J uly 8, 2015. A day I will never forget. I remember it vividly. I lay in bed alone, as my husband was away on business. Donning my earplugs and my eye mask, I said a prayer - over my family in Brazil, my husband, Ricardo, for safe travels, and my two little boys, David and Lucas.

I felt extremely blessed, thinking I had an almost perfect life. And most of all, I was feeling grateful for having the best present a mom could ever hope for—a nanny.

I have a seizure disorder, and since sleep deprivation is one of the main triggers for my episodes, we had hired a nanny to help us through the night so that I could get a full night's rest. Very early on the fateful morning of July 8, I awoke to a muffled but very loud shriek coming from my newborn Lucas's room. As I removed my earplugs and put my eye mask on my forehead, I reached over and grabbed my phone, squinting at the bright display. It was 4:06. I thought, *bottle or diaper?* while wishing my husband was lying beside me since he would always be the one to get up.

Lucas, who was now seven weeks old, had been in the care of this nanny since he was seven days old. The crying stopped for a few minutes, then began again. I kept falling in and out of sleep for what seemed like hours to my sleep-deprived brain. With the sun barely peeking through the curtains, I decided to get out of bed. As I tiptoed on the cold hallway tiles, I looked up and noticed the door to Lucas's room was partially open. I walked over to the doorway and stood and simply observed. My infant was swaddled, tummy side up in his crib, as Shannon placed her hand on his chest and tried moving him side to side while shushing him. Lucas was not having it. Without ever acknowledging my presence or making eye contact with me, she picked him up out of the crib and put him on her shoulder in a burp position. That seemed to stop the screaming, but he was clearly uncomfortable. I came into the bedroom and asked her what was wrong. She very calmly showed me an empty bottle and said she had just finished feeding him. "He is very gassy," she said.

This was not my first rodeo. I had experience with a newborn and knew gassy babies cried a lot. I took Lucas into my arms. As he swung his head backward, he made contorted facial gestures while screeching. I instinctively began rocking and shushing him as well. I didn't know what time it was at that point, but I told the nanny she could go since I was already awake, and Lucas was obviously not going to settle down any time soon. She politely asked if I was sure, I confirmed, and she promptly left my house.

I tiptoed back down the hall to my bedroom with my fussy baby in tow. I unswaddled him and put him on my chest, giving him skin-to-skin contact. He seemed to drift off into sleepy land, which calmed my heart as I thought, *He just wanted his mommy.* With Lucas calm and sleeping, I went back to bed to try and catch the last few zzzs I could get before my older son, David, woke up. After what seemed like only five minutes, I was once again awakened by a jarring shriek. I jumped up and looked at the clock. It was a little past 7:00 a.m. My first thought was, *Okay, you're hungry.* I sat up and attempted to nurse my baby. He was super fussy and would not latch. While I kept trying, I heard another high-pitched sound from down the hall. David, then twenty months old, had woken up.

I put Lucas down on my bed and swaddled him while he screeched like there was no tomorrow. I remember thinking, *Really? Could this day get any worse?* There I was alone, my mom was with her husband, who was about to have cataract surgery, and Lucas would not stop crying—shrieking, really. I put him down in his crib and went to get David. But as I stepped away, the deafening cry got more desperate. I had to pick my infant back up. He finally stopped.

"Fine. You just want to be held," I whispered. Holding Lucas in one arm, I managed to pick up David with my other arm. He was wide awake, smiling and jumping away, with his head of curls bouncing along. I was in no mood to smile back. I proceeded with our morning routine—changed David's diaper, put a clean outfit on him, and fed him breakfast as usual. I plopped down on my spit-up-stained couch with Lucas and was still in a frenzy from the chaotic start on this early day.

Lucas seemed to settle down as I held him in the burp position, his head resting on my shoulder. *Did he really just want to be held?* I wondered. I kept running the scenarios through my head. *What could possibly be upsetting my baby? Colic? Nursing strike? Fever? Infection? Or the nanny's explanation that he was "gassy"?*

But in today's instant-gratification culture, I needed answers, and I needed them now. With cell phone in hand, I summoned Dr. Google to the rescue! After reading many forums and articles, I came to the conclusion that it could literally be all of the above. David, my vibrant, almost-two-year-old, kept pulling at my garments, trying to grab my attention, even when all the while I couldn't put Lucas down.

At around 10:30 a.m., I attempted to nurse Lucas again, and once more, he rejected it. In my distress, the symbolic red flags started waving in my head. I thought, *This is not normal. It has been six hours since his last feeding.* I stood in my living room with my two little ones—David, full of morning energy, bouncing up and down, calling, "Mama! Mama!" and Lucas, letting out a piercing scream. Time just seemed to stop in the chaos around me. I shook it off and decided to put David down for his nap and try to feed Lucas again. Neither plan was working.

The entire time I was texting my husband, who was in between meetings before getting on his flight home. He supported me in my agony, though he couldn't offer much help. I was feeling pretty powerless. The thought of calling my neighbor to come to stay with David briefly crossed my mind. Thankfully, my mom, who had been following [through text messages] the chaos all morning long, offered to come over before I had to beg.

As soon as she walked in the door, I handed Lucas to her so I could call the pediatrician. While I was pacing around my dining room table, waiting for someone to pick up the phone, my mom undressed Lucas, looking for any clues or explanation. Nothing. Meanwhile, the pediatrician's assistant said they had no availability until 3:00 that afternoon. I was adamant. "My baby has been crying since 4:00 a.m. He won't eat, and I need to see someone now!"

She paused and said it would be best to take him to the emergency room.

I glanced at my restless baby. His eyes were rolling back in his head, and his face was turning white as if all the blood had left his body. My mom shook her head and, with a look of complete helplessness, said, "I don't know what's wrong with him, Rachel, but he looks like he's in a lot of pain."

We immediately headed to the ER. My mom sat in the back seat with the boys, keeping her eyes on Lucas while his little hand grasped tightly onto her finger. As soon as the car started moving, both boys dozed off to sleep. I thought, *But of course! Now the doctors will think I'm crazy and completely overreacting.*

We arrived at the hospital, dropped the car off with the valet, and unloaded. Walking in through the automatic glass doors, we were greeted by a perky young lady at the front desk, asking how she could help. I told her my baby had not stopped crying, nor had he eaten since 4:00 a.m. She directed us to a waiting room, where a nurse walked in and took all his vitals. Once again, there was no fever, no ear infection, blood pressure and heartbeat were normal. And, of course, he had stopped crying by then. I expected the doctor to walk in any minute, tell me to give him some Ibuprofen or Tylenol, and go home. I sat on the hospital bed holding Lucas while my mom played with David beside me.

The pediatrician walked in, asked some questions regarding Lucas's symptoms, and then told me to lay Lucas down on the bed. As I did, the doctor walked away but stopped just short of the doorway and stood there with his arms crossed, simply observing for about a minute. It all felt very awkward. Without saying a word and without looking up at me, he walked back in and went straight to the bed.

Pointing behind Lucas's left ear, he looked up at me and asked, "Have you felt this?"

I looked, still not quite sure what he was pointing at, and said no. The doctor took my hand and placed it on what I can only describe as a bulge about the size of my thumb.

"Feel that? That's fluid leaking from his head. We need to do a CT (Computed Tomography) scan right now and find out what kind of fluid it is and where it's coming from. It could be blood; it could be spinal cerebral fluid."

Another ER doctor stood at the door, and he unflinchingly said, "The situation is very serious." He was angry. Not at me, but at the condition this infant was in.

I sat there, mouth agape, in utter shock, as if the world stopped turning for a few moments for me to catch my breath. Suddenly everything changed. Out of nowhere, a flurry of hospital personnel marched into that room, placing wires, sensors, and tubes all over my baby. As they rolled me toward the CT scan room with Lucas in my arms, I glanced at my mom, who had stepped out of the room with David to give everyone space. Everything seemed to be spinning.

My thoughts were reeling in a wave of emotions—shock, fear, unbelief, and confusion, to name a few. Very abruptly, I was brought back to reality when the team of nurses hit the gas and fiercely pushed that hospital bed down the large hallways. I noticed Lucas's right arm twitching and asked the nurse, "Is this normal?"

She looked at me and shook her head no. Then the lightbulb turned on in my head: Left side of the head, right arm twitching—he's having a seizure! I have had seizures since I was five years old, so I'm all too familiar with the medical implications, terminology, and symptoms of this disease. The first sinking thought that came to my mind was, *Oh my God, I passed this on to my son.*

I quickly prayed, *God, please have mercy on Lucas and spare him from living with this disease as I have.* I finished the prayer just as we arrived at the CT scan room. The nurses took Lucas from me and asked me to stand at the corner of the room behind a transparent screen, having me put on what looked like a bulletproof vest. I watched as they put my son on the bed, and he slid into the tube, a sight that was all too familiar to me. I had been down that tube many times in my life. Time seemed to be at hyper speed. We had just barely arrived at the ER, and now they're telling me my baby was in a life-threatening state.

Soon I was approached by one of the doctors, who told me the test was done. He instructed me to wait in the waiting room in the ER, and he would come to talk to me as soon as they had analyzed the results. I walked through the large glass sliding doors, feeling the burst of icy cold air as I exited the room. The deafening stillness was interrupted by irritating beeps, elevator tones, and mindless TV talk shows.

I resisted a suffocating anxiety as I waited. Inside the room, my mom was playing on the floor with David. That little boy didn't have a worry in the world. Looking up, my mom rushed toward me and asked what was happening. I told her everything I knew, and we immediately started praying. We proceeded to text our family members living in Brazil to ask them to pray. By this time, Ricardo was on a plane heading home, having no idea of our distressing situation. After waiting for what seemed like an eternity, two pediatric neurosurgeons walked toward me, papers in hand.

"Mrs. Bruno?" one asked.

I stood up and followed them toward a computer with the CT images on the screen. The look in their eyes said everything. "This is very serious, Mrs. Bruno. Your son has a cranial fracture and an intracerebral blood hemorrhage."

Before I could put my thoughts together, they continued, "Your son is heading to emergency surgery right now." They began handing me paperwork to sign, asking me if I was against blood transfusions. All I remember saying is, "I don't care what you have to do to save my son, save my son." I stood still amidst all the commotion, as all I could see was strangers wheeling my seven-week-old baby into the operating room.

2

He is Mine

I stood there motionless. My heart was pounding, and yet I felt emotionally frozen. Still trying to comprehend what was going on, I walked toward the waiting room. *Cranial fracture? A newborn's skull isn't completely fused yet ... one of those fissures must have popped open. Intracerebral blood hemorrhage? Like an aneurysm?* So many questions raced through my mind, yet it never crossed my mind that this could have been done intentionally.

I called the nanny to see if I could get any clarification. She did not answer her phone. I called the secondary number I had for her, and an older gentleman picked up.

"Is Shannon available?" I asked.

"No," he replied.

"Can you please ask her to call Rachel as soon as possible? Thank you."

I sat down with my mom and overly tired David, who was awake way past his nap time. The silence between my mom and me was deafening as each of us prayed, trying to make sense of everything that had just happened. We were texting our friends all over the country and relatives in Brazil to pray for Lucas as he went into surgery.

While texting mid-sentence, my phone rang. It was Shannon. I stood up and walked over to a corner of the room.

"Remember all the fussing this morning with Lucas?" I asked her.

"Um-hum," she replied.

"Turns out he has a cranial fracture and a blood hemorrhage," I explained.

"Oh, my God! Is he going to be okay?" she asked.

"They just took him in for emergency surgery. I don't know ... did anything happen last night?" I asked.

"Nothing out of the ordinary. He was really gassy all night," she said.

"So, nothing happened to his head? Maybe he hit it against the crib?" I asked.

"No. Do you need me to bring you food to the hospital? Or someone to watch David?" she said.

"No, that's okay. My mom is here," I replied.

"Please keep me updated! I'm going to call my prayer group right now and ask everyone to keep little Lucas in their prayers," she said.

"Okay. Thank you," I said and then hung up.

I hung up the phone thinking, *Yeah, all we can do right now is pray.*

Honestly, I can't remember what I did during the four hours of surgery. It's all a big blur to me. I do remember seeing my last name change colors on the monitors in the waiting room and the status of the procedure switching to "Complete."

My heart started racing once again as I anticipated what news the doctor would be coming with. Good or bad? I wondered.

Shortly, I saw the doctor approaching in his white lab coat, clipboard and paperwork in hand. He said, "Everything went according to plan. We were able to suction out most of the blood, and we placed a sugar plate to repair the fracture." From what I understood, a sugar plate was made of a dissolvable material that would eventually "fade away" as his cranium grew. It was a temporary solution for now.

"Is he going to be okay? Is there any brain damage?" I asked.

"It's too soon to know. He will be in observation in the Pediatric Intensive Care Unit (PICU). We don't even know if he will survive the next forty-eight hours."

As those words sank into my head, a quiet voice spoke in my heart—*He is Mine. I gave him to you.* At that moment, I was transported back three years before when my first pregnancy ended in a miscarriage. I had prayed so vehemently for these babies; I had wanted children so much. With the miscarriage, my world had changed. My priorities shifted as it occurred to me that I might not be able to carry a baby to full term. And then I remembered the Bible verse in David's picture book—"In my distress I cried out to the LORD; yes, I prayed to my God for help. He heard me from his sanctuary; my cry to him reached his ears" (Psalm 18:6 NLT).

"Do you have any other questions?" the doctor asked.

"No," I replied. I had peace.

"Then let me take you up to his room," the doctor said.

As I walked into the PICU, I could see faces filled with pain, anguish, confusion, and heartache through the glass doors that surrounded the rooms. Then I saw Lucas, his head covered in white gauze, with EEG wires sticking out of every orifice you can imagine. Two PICC (peripherally inserted central catheter) lines, a breathing tube, and a feeding tube invaded his little body. The endless beeping of hospital equipment encircling Lucas's bed drowned out my own quiet sobbing.

I was too scared to touch him. All I could see was a seemingly lifeless baby in a medically induced coma. I thought of the Bible verse again, and in tears, I prayed, "Please God, don't take him away from me. If I have to dedicate the rest of my life to taking care of this child, I will. Just don't take him away from me."

I immediately heard it again: *He is mine.* And the peace that surpasses all understanding filled my heart. (Philippians 4:7)

The neurosurgeon was still standing by my side and tried to comfort me as best he could. "I've seen cases worse than this where the child ended up having no brain damage ... then again, I've seen cases less severe where the child had severe brain damage. We will be closely monitoring him for the next forty-eight hours. He is stable and doing very well at this time."

I thanked him and shook his hand as he stepped away to care for the other patients. I gazed at Lucas once more, took a deep breath, and settled into the room. I had done the one thing I could do for Lucas at this point—I had prayed, and God gave me peace. Now all I could do was wait. I put my bag down, sat on the fold-out couch, and immediately began thinking about logistics.

David had been up all day without a nap and was getting understandably cranky. By this time, it was well past four o'clock in the afternoon. I had been up since four in the morning and had not had one bite to eat. I obviously wasn't leaving the hospital that night.

I finally spoke to my husband when he was on a layover in Arizona. Hearing his voice, I couldn't hold back my tears. "Ricardo, he's just lying here. The doctors don't know whether he will survive the next forty-eight hours. David hasn't slept all day. I have no way of taking him home … my mom is here. Marty just had his cataract surgery and is home alone …"

He listened to me spew all my thoughts to him in random order until I broke down, crying to the point that I couldn't speak.

Calmly, Ricardo said, "He's in God's hands, Rachel. Lucas has brought us so much joy, and he will continue to bring us joy for years to come. Everything is going to be okay."

His words immediately quieted my heart, bringing me back to the place of God, a place of peace. A place of *He is Mine*. I hung up the phone, collapsed into my mom's arms, and cried.

Not a minute later, one of my best friends, Tatiana, showed up at the hospital. As soon as our eyes met, we embraced each other and wept. I can only imagine the sight of us three, just weeping. Such a tragic moment, but at the same time, such love between us. Tati, as I called her, is like the sister I never had. She knew my story—the miscarriage, the surgeries, and the seizures she had witnessed, to name a few. She knew my pain as a friend and as a mom herself.

After we had a moment to grieve and comfort each other, we simultaneously went into mommy-planning mode. Tati looked at David and my mom and began to shoot rapid-fire questions.

"How are they getting home? Where are you spending the night? Where is David going to go? Where is Ricardo? How long is Lucas going to be here? Have you had dinner?" All obvious questions, which hadn't crossed my mind. It was close to eight o'clock at night now.

I asked her if she could take my mom and David home. I would spend the night at the hospital, and Ricardo would come straight from the airport later that night.

I said my goodbyes to my mom and David. I hugged and kissed David goodnight. I told him to be a good boy for *Adede* (a word he made up for Grandma) and that I loved him. He left happy as can be, knowing he would be spending the night at Grandma's house where he could get away with anything. It made me smile. People say you never know when it's the last time you're doing something. This was one of those moments.

I hugged Tati and thanked her as she waved and went down the hall, leaving those cold walls behind. Stray agonizing shrieks penetrated the walls; moaning sounds echoed through the hall.

Everyone is so vulnerable in these see-through cages. What a crazy day, I thought. I felt like I was in some surreal human art exhibit, except instead of sightseers taking photos, there were medical residents and fellows taking detailed notes.

My brain felt completely detached from all sensations as I observed my sedated, unconscious son. Although my heart was breaking at the thought of what might happen to Lucas within the next forty-eight hours, I kept rationalizing the situation in an attempt to console myself. *At least the doctors were able to do something ... he's in a good hospital ... thank God for my mom ... David is safe and sleeping ... Lucas will be just fine.*

Quite abruptly, my introspection was interrupted by a knock on the glass door. I looked up and saw an officer in uniform. It was around 9 p.m.

He slid the door open and asked, "May I come in?"

Caught completely off guard, I nodded. "Yes, please."

Then behind him, a lady with a very calm demeanor stepped in as well.

He introduced himself as Officer Locker. "Are you the mother? We just want to ask you a few questions about what happened. Is that okay?"

"Yes," I replied.

"What happened to your son was worse than getting struck in the head by a bullet," the officer said. "We want to help you figure out how this happened to your son. Will you help us?"

At this point, I figured if they were asking me for help, they most certainly were gathering information about the nanny. When I pictured what the officer described, "a bullet" striking my son's head, I couldn't help but think of the insinuation that he thought someone tried to kill my son. What else would a bullet to the head be?

The lady introduced herself as Dora, a social worker for Orange County. She sat on the pullout sofa beside me and seemed very empathetic, stating how sorry she was that this happened to my son and how hard it must be for me.

I nodded and even smiled in appreciation.

She asked me how I was feeling, and I said I was doing as well as I could under the circumstances. I was trying not to get emotional, as I figured that would not help since these people were trying to gather information and help. I began to tell the same story I had told the neurosurgeon earlier. "He was with the nanny … I heard the scream …"

Officer Locker, leaning on the wall, interrupted me. "Why did you wait so long to bring him to the hospital?"

I replied, "Because I didn't know what was happening. He just wouldn't stop crying." In my mind, I was thinking, *Have you ever had a newborn, sir? They cry a lot.*

Dora stopped him and said, "Yes, I understand. Did he have any symptoms the night before?"

The questioning continued for more than two hours. I can't recall all the questions verbatim. I do, however, remember feeling as if Officer Locker was insinuating my guilt when he asked questions like, "Why did you bring him to a hospital in Orange County when you live in LA County? Why didn't you call 911?"

And I just kept repeating, "Because I didn't know what was wrong with him. The nanny told me he was gassy."

Dora, meanwhile, wanted to be the peacemaker, always bringing the discussion back to the children. The last question she asked was if I had any other children. I told her I had David, who was twenty months old. She asked me where he was and if she could go "take a look" at him.

I looked at the wall clock in the room; it was close to 10:00 p.m. I told her David was at my mother's house, most likely asleep by now. She assured me they would not wake him. She said she just wanted to make sure he was all right. I found it odd that she wanted to see David; what did he have to do with anything? Then again, I thought they were gathering information so they could question the nanny.

I called my mom and explained to her what was going on. I informed her that the social worker, Dora, would be stopping by to see David. My mom complied, and I gave Dora my mother's address. She thanked me for my cooperation and stepped outside the room with Officer Locker. I could see them talking to each other through the now-infamous glass doors. Ricardo had landed at LAX and phoned me. I brought him up to date on Lucas's and David's status, then told him there was a police officer and a social worker standing outside my door. I expressed my confusion as I had no idea why these people were there or who told them to come.

He told me to cooperate and that he would be on his way to the hospital after making a quick stop at home to pick up my seizure medications. Meanwhile, Dora left, and Officer Locker continued to pace up and down the hall. He was talking on his phone, to whom or about what, only God knows. Afterward, he came back into the room and asked me where the father was. I told him he had been on a business trip but was on his way to the hospital from LAX as we spoke.

He inquired when Ricardo had left, and I told him two days ago. Locker meticulously jotted everything down on his clipboard. He then asked me about the nanny. I gave him all the information I had—name, address, and phone number.

I felt pretty confident, thinking, *Okay, they've gotten everything they can out of me. Now they are going to question the nanny.* Remember, I had been up since 4:00 in the morning; it was now close to 11:00 at night, and I was absolutely exhausted—mentally, physically, and emotionally. I just wanted to hug my husband and get some rest.

At that very moment, I received a text message from Ricardo, saying he had arrived in the hospital. I stood in the hallway and saw him coming through the double doors, only to be stopped by Officer Locker along the way.

They began talking as Ricardo tried to make eye contact with me and walked toward Lucas's room. Officer Locker stepped aside and let Ricardo see his son. Without hesitation, he then pulled Ricardo aside and asked if he could talk to him in the other room. Ricardo looked at me, and I shrugged my shoulders to imply, Go ahead! It was past eleven o'clock at night by now.

After about thirty minutes, Ricardo came back to Lucas's room with Officer Locker, who proceeded to explain to both of us, "What happened to your son is as serious as someone being shot." He went on to say that the amount of force it takes to break someone's skull makes it a very serious offense. At no point did he tell me I that was a suspect, I was facing criminal charges, and that this was a child abuse investigation. As we spoke to Officer Locker, two detectives, Cross and Sword, walked in and asked if they could talk to me.

We walked over to another room, where Detective Cross made it a point to tell me this was "not an interrogation," but simply a conversation. I complied once again and lay on the vinyl bench. Physically and emotionally drained, I observed that this room felt very different, with white walls and a solid door with a lock. No glass here. The detectives said they were going to step out for a minute and would be right back.

At this point, my body began to remind me that I have seizures. I start feeling what I refer to as *flashes*, or what medical professionals call *auras*—a sort of warning someone's body gives right before a seizure. Sleep deprivation is a major trigger for my seizures.

That is why we had decided to get a nanny for our newborn. It had been almost two years since I had my last seizure; prior to that, it took nearly twenty years to get them controlled by medication, and I was not about to jeopardize my treatment. I lay there waiting, praying to God to please keep the seizures away.

Then I heard a gentle door knock as the detectives came back into the room and closed the door. Detective Cross was slim and had her dark hair pulled back into a bun. I don't remember what Detective Sword looked like since she barely said a word throughout the entire questioning. Detective Cross was very sympathetic, just as social worker Dora had been. She told me how sorry she was to have to do this but thanked me for helping with the investigation and showing I truly cared about my son's well-being.

I began telling the same story for what seemed like the hundredth time in a single day. It was almost 2:00 in the morning. I had been sleep-deprived essentially for twenty-four hours. Although I can't remember the line of questioning verbatim, I just remember saying over and over, "I don't know what happened." I couldn't bring myself to make an accusation about someone when I truly didn't know what had happened.

Officer Locker's words lingered in my head: "as serious as a gunshot." *Was the nanny trying to kill my baby? Do I know "beyond a reasonable doubt" that this was the case? No.* I didn't. Therefore, I wouldn't speculate.

Detective Cross questioned me for about two hours. One particular question stood out to me; she asked what I think should happen to caregivers who abuse their subjects.

I had held it together all day, and I just couldn't anymore. My voice began to crack, my eyes welling with tears as I answered, "They should be put on some type of list like the sexual abusers are."

She tilted her head as if amused by my reaction. "Why does that make you emotional?"

I responded, "When someone has the title of caregiver, it makes you trust them—someone who is going to care for your loved one. A person like this doesn't deserve this title. I trusted her when I obviously shouldn't have."

At that point, I practically begged the detectives to please let me go so I could sleep. I was having flashes and didn't want to induce a seizure. They quickly gathered up their paperwork and told me we could continue tomorrow if I was willing to help.

I told them yes. My head would probably be much better tomorrow. I walked out of that "conversation room," feeling like a zombie. My husband was waiting for me in the room with Lucas. He knew my medical condition and immediately gave me my medication, telling me to sleep. I lay on the vinyl-covered mattress in Lucas's room and put my eye mask on and earplugs in. Too exhausted to even pray, I just moaned something to the effect of, "God, be with us," and dozed off.

Unbeknownst to me, Ricardo was covering up a horrible occurrence that had happened just minutes before while the detectives were questioning me. Something I wouldn't find out until I awoke the next morning. Little did I know that when I kissed David goodbye earlier that night, it was literally to bid farewell to my twenty-month-old firstborn son. What would happen in the next twenty-four hours … no one could have ever imagined.

3

Taken

I remember waking up on July 9, 2015, to beeping sounds from the hospital monitors. I opened my eyes, and my husband was sitting in a rocking chair, just staring at me. I could tell from his expression that something was terribly wrong.

I jumped out of the pull-out bed the hospital provided to see if Lucas was still there. He was. Hooked up just like he was the night before. He was fine.

"What happened?" I asked.

"They took David," Ricardo, who had slept on a bench at the hospital, said.

"What do you mean, they took David?! Where? Who? What?"

I soon learned that the previous night, while the detectives were questioning me, the social worker, Dora, along with three law enforcement officers, had gone to my mom's house at 2 a.m. I called my mom immediately to hear the words out of her mouth.

They had knocked on my mom's door, saying they wanted to check on David, which my mom had prepared for nearly five hours earlier. When Dora left the hospital after speaking to me the night before, I assumed she was on her way to my mom's house at that moment. It turns out that was not the case. My mom said Dora took a walk through their house, looked in the refrigerator, then asked where David was sleeping. As soon as she walked into the room where David was asleep, she turned on the light, waking him up. My mom said David smiled at her and jumped straight up, full of energy, thinking it was playtime. He had no bruises, no scars, no sign of abuse whatsoever. As I was on my way to sleep the previous night, Dora was telling my mom she was being "ordered" to take David.

My mom was in shock and wouldn't comply, saying this was not what they said they would do. To further intimidate my mom, Dora told her if she didn't hand David over, they would arrest her. Three police officers, including Officer Locker, just stood there and said nothing.

"I'm calling backup," Dora said as she saw her previous attempts at coercion were not shifting the needle.

My mom asked, "If I go to jail, can I take him [David] with me?"

Dora told her, "No, he would go to foster care. And if you get arrested, you will not be eligible to care for him, for you will have a criminal record." Again, the police officers standing right there never said a word.

My mom felt she had no choice but to do what they said.

Dora told my mom she couldn't wait any longer, and she would have to forcefully take David from my mom's arms. My mom began to panic, not knowing what to do. David began crying, sensing the chaos. He knew something was wrong.

My stepdad, Marty, was in the garage—mind you, it's 2 a.m.—looking through his phone book, trying to find attorneys. No one answered his calls. Finally, my mom gave David to Dora. He screamed in despair as she took him out of the house and headed to the minivan.

David was kicking and screaming, to the point that the social worker couldn't get him into the car seat, and she asked for my mother's assistance. My mom was forced to buckle David in while he screamed and cried for her help.

My mom told me this scenario over the phone as I sat with my unconscious baby in the hospital. We were both sobbing as I heard it for the first time, and she had to relive it again. I couldn't fathom what my mom had gone through, having to witness David being torn away and not being able to do a darn thing. She said she stood on the sidewalk and cried. For the first time, she had seen my stepfather cry. In a matter of minutes, social services and law enforcement were off, taking my twenty-month-old son to who knows where.

Ricardo had been on the phone with my mom during this entire ordeal, begging Dora not to do this. He knew all this when he had told me to go to sleep after my interview with the detectives, but he protected me, at least while he could.

Now he was telling me this story in tears. He had desperately tried to convince the social worker and law enforcement not to take David. I was crying in pain at the thought of my mom, David, and now my husband. I was crying at the betrayal I felt from the police officers, the detectives, the social worker. These people told me they were there to help me. They lied to me. Had it really been their intent to seize my son all along? I cried with self-doubt, thinking, *I should have never said anything to Dora about David. Where he was, who he was with. This can't be legal. There must be some misunderstanding.*

And now, at around 10:00 a.m. on July 9, the day after we had brought Lucas to the hospital, we didn't know where David was. Dora wasn't answering our calls; neither was her office nor her supervisor.

It was a day of sheer pain. All we did was cry, pleading God to show us the way. After a few hours of "letting it all out," we had to put on our thinking caps. We decided to divide and conquer. Ricardo called social services while I called attorneys.

Ricardo got no response from social services. After about ten attempts, I found an attorney who practiced family law and specialized in juvenile cases. His name was Art, and I spoke with him over the phone that Friday morning. He told me he knew where my son was and to meet him at his office at noon. In the meantime, he told me to contact as many people as I could to write character letters for me. I still couldn't wrap my brain around what the heck was going on. I mean, really, *What was going on?*

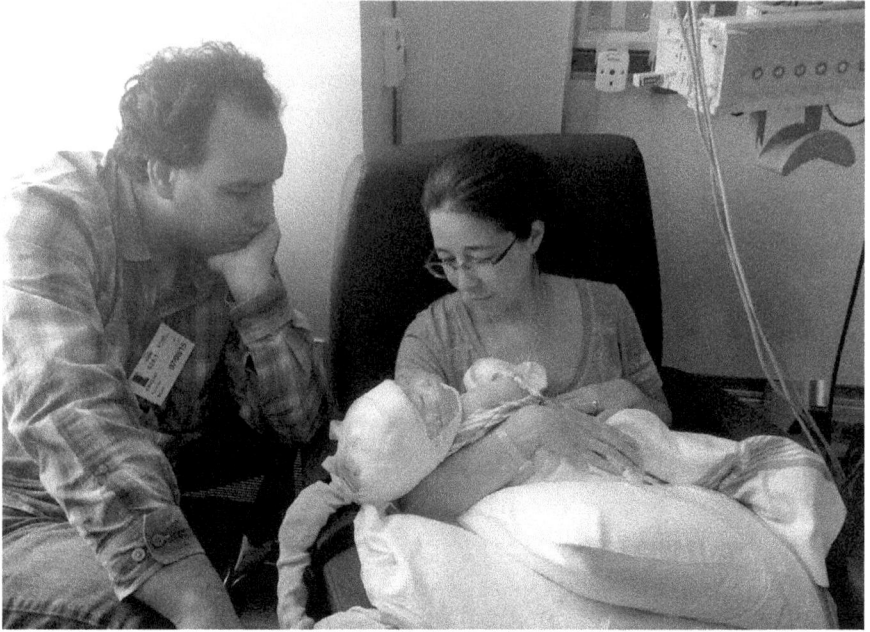

4

Lawyering Up

I arrived at Art's office, and the first thing I asked was, "Where is my son, and when do I go get him?"

He was very nonchalant, "I know where he is." He lifted his hand, showing me his pointer finger, signaling "give me a minute."

He picked up the phone and dialed a number on speed dial. He said, "My name is Art LaCilento. I'm representing Rachel Bruno, mother of a minor. Can you check if he's there?"

Sure enough, they had taken my son to the county's children's shelter known as Orangewood. I breathed a sigh of relief. "So when can I go pick him up?" I said with a giggle.

"No," Art replied. "He's under protective custody. You can't pick him up until the court decides where he's going."

He must not be understanding, I thought. I had explained to him on the phone they had taken my son without my consent, with no proof whatsoever. And now I didn't know where he was. "This is absurd!"

"Yeah," he said, "they can do that."

"What? What do you mean 'they can do that!?'" I said, again with a giggle but mixed with befuddlement. "How the heck could they get away with this?! Don't we have a Constitution?! What about my rights?!"

He stopped me in the middle of my rant, looked me straight in the eye, and told me, "You have no idea what you're in for. Stay here. He walked across the hallway and brought in a woman (whom I later found out was his wife) and said, "Tell her!"

I turned my head and looked toward her, not understanding what Art was getting at. She said, "Yes, they can take away your children. They do it all the time."

Art continued, "What happened to your son Lucas is criminal. You are facing fifteen years in jail and a $100,000 bond if they decide to charge you."

"What?" I replied. "I didn't do this!"

"Doesn't matter."

"What do you mean it doesn't matter? What about the nanny?"

"They may investigate her; they may not. But right now, they have your children, and they are not going to give them back to you."

"What are you talking about? I DIDN'T DO THIS!"

At this point, he was visibly frustrated with me and repeated, "Listen to me, this is family court. They do not follow Constitutional law. They can do whatever they deem is 'in the best interest of the child.' You need to call this private investigator and a counseling center. Enroll in their child abuse class, parenting class, and get ready for court."

I felt like I had just gotten run over by a freight train. I couldn't process what I was hearing. All I kept thinking was, *But I didn't do anything! What about the nanny?!*

He called the court clerk right there in front of me, who informed us that our court hearing would be on Monday, July 13. My husband would have to get his own lawyer to avoid a conflict of interest.

Art reiterated once again, "They're not going to give your children back to you. You are undergoing a criminal investigation. Your husband cannot defend you, or they will say he doesn't have your children's best interests at heart. Unless we find someone to take them in, David and Lucas will be going to foster care. If the case lasts longer than six months, and they will make it last longer than six months, they can be legally adopted by their foster family.

"What?! ADOPTED?" I shrieked.

He continued, "Your saving grace is that your husband was out of town when this happened. Legally speaking, he wasn't even at the crime scene. Your best bet is to ask the judge to give sole custody to your husband. That way they don't even risk going into foster care. If the judge grants this request, they're going to kick you out of your house.

"What? I'm not going to be able to see them? But—"

"I don't want you talking to *anybody*! You understand?! Nobody! I want you to get as many character letters as you can, especially from doctors and people who aren't family, so we can take them to court on Monday."

Just as he said that, my gynecologist, whom I had called earlier that day, called me back. I began crying as I explained the situation to her.

She said, "I'm so sorry, Rachel, it's not even in your character to do such a thing." Not only did she know my medical history, the miscarriage, and the surgeries she had performed, she also knew how much I wanted these babies. She assured me she would write me a character letter.

As I hung up the phone, I saw a little glimpse of humanity in my feisty attorney for the first time. He reached out, touched my hand, and said, "I believe you."

I wiped my tears away, feeling a sense of comfort that I so needed at that moment.

He then continued, "Call the nanny and tell her that her services are no longer needed, *not a word more*. I want you to get as many character letters as you can so we can take them to court on Monday. Do *whatever* the social workers tell you to do. Don't argue, and *do not* talk to them anymore about this case. I don't want you talking to anyone in law enforcement—not the police, not the detectives—without me being present."

Before I left his office, I had one thing I just could not get off my chest. "Is there any way we can see David? What if I just show up? What are they going to do to me?"

"You don't step foot on that property! If you go there, they will tell the judge you are not complying with the court's order, which will immediately put a 'stain' on your record. Let me make some phone calls, and I'll get back to you."

I was beginning to realize there was something much more sinister going on. I got back to the hospital to explain everything to Ricardo. My head was still swirling in disbelief as I kept praying God would save our family from this situation. I kept waiting for someone to call and say this was all one big mistake. That phone call never came.

What did come was a call from Art, telling me social services was giving me and Ricardo permission to visit David on-site at the county's children's shelter for thirty minutes the next day, Saturday morning.

Meanwhile, Lucas was in the Pediatric ICU being monitored 24/7, still in a medically induced coma. I had not been able to hold him due to all the wires and equipment coming out of him. So much had happened within forty-eight hours. My brain couldn't process all the emotions; my heart couldn't bear all the pain; my body felt like it was floating and just going through the motions on autopilot. Toward the end of those critical forty-eight hours for Lucas, I got on my knees that night and asked God again to please not take my baby away. The Holy Spirit whispered to me again, "He is Mine."

Ricardo and I got ready the following morning to go see David, not knowing what to expect, but nothing could have prepared us for what we were about to experience.

5

My David, No Longer the Boy I Knew

We arrived at what seemed like an apartment complex with small housing units. I walked up to the front door to see a stranger holding my son in her arms. I reached out to hold him, excitedly saying, "Hi, David!" and he just stared at me. Not a smile, not a word. His big round eyes, so confused, but I couldn't say anything. Social services had made our visit contingent on the fact that we could not talk about the case, and could only communicate in English.

David was only twenty months old and just beginning to speak. At home, we spoke exclusively Portuguese with him since we wanted him to be able to communicate with his family in Brazil when he got older. He probably had no idea what any of us were saying to him, making this visit even more confusing and traumatic. I held back the tears and smiled.

The lady put him down, and he stood there, again confused. She walked into the "house" and gestured for him to follow. She told me he hadn't slept very well the previous night, and he hadn't eaten anything. I thought, *Well, duh! The poor kid was taken kicking and screaming from his grandma's house to sleep in a strange place with complete strangers! What did you expect?*

I said, "What did you try to feed him?"

And she said, "Peas and hot dogs."

And as stupid as it sounds, that was painful to hear. I'd never fed my son a hot dog in his life. In his entire two years. I had made all the food at home

27

from scratch. I felt so violated. All the decisions I had made to raise my son, down to the foods he would eat, were being ripped away from me. It was a feeling I just couldn't describe.

We—as a family unit—were all so traumatized at that moment. We had been violated as a family, and our communication had been severed. Our assurance had been breached, as we were now being watched by a stranger who could decide our fate. I got down on the floor to play with David, and he slowly got closer to me.

Ricardo started playing with him, and he began to open up. He began to laugh and smile. The ever-present social worker was like a helicopter around us. He sat on my lap, and I hugged and kissed him. When I was finally regaining his trust and we all kind of had our guard down, enjoying each other's company, the social worker spoke up and informed us our thirty minutes were up.

That turned out to be the most heartbreaking thirty minutes of my life. I will never forget that pain … *ever.* My heart was pounding, and I was holding back tears. How was I supposed to leave my baby yet again? I couldn't put him down, and the social worker kept repeating herself. "I'm sorry, ma'am, but your time is up. You have to go."

I remember placing David on the floor and kneeling beside him, telling him in Portuguese, "Mommy and Daddy have to go now, okay?" His eyes immediately widened, filling with tears, and he grabbed my leg, trying to climb up on me like a tree.

I stood up. "We'll be back soon, okay?" I told him. He was glued to my leg and wouldn't let go. He started crying hysterically.

All that kept going through my head was, *I said goodbye to my son at the hospital two days ago, and then I disappeared. Now I had shown up again, and I had to disappear again.*

David started screaming, "No, Mommy, no!" He wouldn't let go of my leg, and I couldn't move, my body visibly shaking at this point. I couldn't hold back the crying.

The social worker picked him up and told him, "Say bye-bye," while waving her hand.

Ricardo's hands were shaking, and as he cried, we looked at each other, held hands, and turned our backs to the sound of our twenty-month-old baby screaming his heart out while we walked away. The sound of my son screaming, "Mamae, mamae!" and not being able to do anything will be forever scarred in my heart. Ricardo and I held hands and sobbed like two school-aged children walking towards our car, hearing the screaming fade as we got further and further away.

We entered the car and bawled our eyes out as we held each other. It was the most painful, most heart-wrenching experience I have ever had. We must have sat there in the parking lot crying for at least thirty minutes. We held each other's hands and prayed together out loud, imploring God–begging Him–to help us make these judges see how unjust this was. How wrong they were. To make the children's lawyers read our character letters. To let them understand that we did not harm our children. We asked that our family be back together and that God would please have mercy on our children and our family. In Jesus' name.

I never felt so helpless.

We went back to the hospital, and I called Art to tell him we had just gone to see David. He had been working behind the scenes and asked if I had any family the boys could stay with if the court decided to remove them. I told him my mom and stepdad were my only family here, and they'd be willing to keep them.

"Great," he said. "A caseworker will visit your mom's house and make sure they pass a home safety evaluation. If so, most likely, your children will go to them."

I must remind you, my reader, all this happened before I ever stepped foot in a courtroom. At that point, the hours went by, the days went by, and it was all the same nightmare to me. I had no sense of time anymore, just that my life was in limbo at the mercy of a judge who would decide our fate on July 13.

I spent the entire weekend scouring my phone for contacts, specifically for doctors, classmates, work colleagues—anyone who wasn't family. Art said to get letters from people who had known me throughout my entire life. I immediately remembered some key people who were from the church and had known me from my mother's womb. My dad was a pastor in Brazil, and when missionaries traveled to our state from the U.S., he was one of the only pastors who could speak English, and he often translated for the American pastors. One such pastor was Robert Goree with his wife, Helen. They were there when my dad's church in Brazil was inaugurated, which also happened to be the day I was born.

My father was tragically killed in a drunk-driving accident when I was nine months old, but the Gorees never forgot my mom and me. The First Assembly of God, which Pastor Goree pastored in Fremont, California, had sponsored us to move to the States while my mom attended Bible school. Now, more than thirty years later, Pastor Goree had gone to be with the Lord, and I hadn't spoken to Helen, his wife, in years. I decided to call her, feeling such anxiety and some shame, thinking, What would Helen think of me? I should have known to shut down those thoughts.

She answered the phone and was as classy and lovely as I remembered her. I told her I needed her help and immediately began to cry … "They took my children … my baby is in the hospital, and they don't know whether he's going to live … they think I did it!"

She stopped me and, in a composed voice, replied, "Oh, Rachel, I'm so sorry. What a horrible situation. Let's pray." Once she had prayed and I had calmed down, she asked, "What do you need?"

I explained the character letters needed for the judge, and she said, "Of course I will write you a character letter. When do you need it by?"

Time and time again, this was the response I got from so many people. I obtained twenty-three character letters during the weekend before court on Monday. The letters were written by people who ranged from lifelong friends to college acquaintances to medical professionals. I thought there was no way a judge could read these letters and still think I had abused my sons. Our primary pediatrician went as far as to say he would "stake his career" on us as parents.

What I'm about to say sounds inconceivable, but I never felt so loved, so grateful. You're probably reading this and thinking, Gratitude?! Grateful for *what?! Your children have just been taken away, you're being falsely accused, and you're grateful?!* This transformation of my mind and heart was a move by the Holy Spirit, which would be a continuing thread throughout this journey.

6

Happy Anniversary

July 12, 2015, was our twelfth wedding anniversary. We spent it in the hospital with Lucas and on the phones with our respective lawyers, trying to figure out the strategy for our hearing the next day.

Little by little, as my friends came to visit the hospital, I began feeling human again. In the midst of all this despair, I felt so loved. The Bible gives us this promise: "No trial has overtaken you that is not faced by others. And God is faithful: He will not let you be tried beyond what you are able to bear, but with the trial will also provide a way out so that you may be able to endure it" (1 Corinthians 10:13).

God sent many people to hold my hand so that I would "be able to endure it." Even in the immense pain my heart was feeling, I also had a tremendous sense of peace—one that surpasses all understanding (Philippians 4:7). I knew Lucas would ultimately be okay. What I did not know, however, was whether my sons would be reunited with me. Was I going to go to jail? And if so, when was any or all of this going to happen? This is where I had to rely completely on my faith and trust God.

I also felt small but in a good way. Who am I that all these people would stand up for me? Friends, like Aline and John, who would bring me meals every night at the hospital? Friends who would cry with me. Pray for me. Encourage me. Little Bible nuggets from childhood would pop up in my head: "A friend loves at all times, and a brother is born for a time of adversity"

(Proverbs 17:17). And I had many "brothers" during this entire process. I will be forever grateful to them.

My mom convinced us to at least have lunch on our anniversary, and she would stay with Lucas at the hospital. Upon returning, we were greeted by a doctor informing us he was going to remove Lucas's head covering. I had not seen my baby look "normal" since the surgery. The critical forty-eight hours had passed, they had found the right cocktail of medications to control his seizures, and now we would see how the wound was healing.

The doctor slowly cut the gauze, carefully removing it and revealing a scar that began at the top of his hairline and followed all the way down behind his ear, making an inverted C shape around his head. It was quite jarring to look at. There were still remnants of blue marker where the surgeons had made their incisions. Half of his head was shaved, and the other half was full of the luscious, dark locks he had been born with. His eyes were closed, and his face was swollen. He had tubes coming out of his nose and mouth and a drain on his head, "catching" excess blood from the surgery.

Ricardo and I stood by his bedside, holding hands, tears streaming down our cheeks at this shocking sight of our baby. The doctor assured us that he looked "good." The scar was healing well, he didn't have any excess blood in the drain, and he would soon be "waking up" as they stopped giving him the sedatives.

The doctors walked out, and shortly after, a nurse came in, asking if I would like to hold Lucas. The last time I had held him was in the emergency room three days earlier. I nodded yes, and sat on a rocker beside his hospital bed. The nurse carefully untangled all the tubes and wires, picked him up, and brought him to me. I held my baby and cried. To feel that little body next to mine—something so simple yet something I had taken for granted—it was almost as if I was holding him for the first time again. I kissed his head and thanked God my baby was alive. What an incredible experience to witness a living miracle.

My friends John and Aline were there with us, not a dry eye in that room but complete silence, as we all revered the moment we were witnessing. It was nothing but a pure miracle. That day just so happened to be his "monthversary." Lucas was now officially two months old. I received a FaceTime call from my family in Brazil. There they were, the family from my mom's side, my dad's side, and my husband's side. They were all gathered at my grandpa's house, holding a birthday cake and singing "Happy Birthday to Lucas."

It was a room filled with joy in one of the saddest places one could be—a children's hospital intensive care unit. We laughed and exchanged virtual kisses and hugs. Everyone encouraged us and our "little warrior." Once again, a moment like this instilled in me a sense of God's faithfulness. Those who mattered most knew me, knew my character, and never once doubted me. I had twenty-three letters to prove it.

Back at my mom's house, the social services agency contacted her and told her she had received clearance to pick up David from the shelter that evening, but my husband and I still could not see him. My heart was heavy, but again, at peace, knowing that David was now with my mom. He had spent two nights and three days at the children's shelter. Later, the social worker met with my mom at her house to sign some paperwork. She informed my mom that everything would ultimately be decided at the hearing on Monday. But if things didn't go according to plan (reunification), would she be willing to adopt both my sons?

My mom nearly fell off her seat. She thought, *"What?! Why would I adopt my grandsons?! No!"*

The social worker went on with her script, stating that if my mom did not adopt them, then they would be adopted by a foster family. She further enticed my mom by saying she'd be eligible to receive $670/month per child from the government, along with WIC ("Women, Infants, and Children," a California Department of Public Health program), and all the social welfare programs available in California, if she became the adoptive parent.

My mom responded, "I don't want your money. I want you to give them back to their parents, to whom they rightfully belong!"

Again, the social worker tried to appease my mom, stating this would only be temporary and was simply a proactive step before the hearing on Monday. Meaning he could either enforce an adoption order or have the children reunited with us. I will remind you once again that all this was being done before I ever stepped into a courtroom. My mom reluctantly signed the paperwork and was approved to be David's and Lucas's official foster parent. Although Lucas was still in the hospital, his status was yet to be determined since we didn't know how long he would be staying there.

7

Judgment Day

It was July 13, 2015, and finally, the court day had arrived. Monday morning, bright and early at 8 a.m., Ricardo and I were at the courthouse. My parents had to come in a separate car, as they had David, and we were not allowed to be around him without supervision. As Ricardo and I walked toward the courthouse from the parking lot, my mom walked up and handed me a small piece of paper she had folded in her hand with tears in her eyes. I opened it, and it was a handwritten note: "Do not fear, for I am with you; do not be afraid, for I am your God. I will strengthen you; I will surely help you; I will uphold you with My right hand of righteousness" (Isaiah 41:10). I hugged her, knowing we were all going to be praying in the spirit inside our minds.

I had not seen my lawyer since our initial meeting. He came that morning, with his twin brother, who also happened to be a lawyer and had been retained for Ricardo. The brothers pulled us aside to discuss strategy. With their twenty-plus years of experience in family court and working alongside social services, both lawyers agreed that the social services agency would not give the children back to me. They said our only alternative was to request that full (temporary) custody be granted solely to the father. I really had no choice—it was between my sons getting placed with strangers and getting adopted or legally being solely their father's. Then my lawyer reminded me the one caveat to this "deal:" I would be evicted from my house indefinitely until social services and the police finished their "investigation." I would have to complete their "safety plan" in the time allotted, and in future hearings the case would be reassessed accordingly.

Once again, I felt like I had been hit by a bulldozer. "What do you mean indefinitely? Am I not going to be able to see them? Where am I supposed to live? What about the nanny?"

Art looked at me, rather irritated, and said, "I already went through this with you! Your children are under two years old and nonverbal! These people pounce on them like vultures. This is your best bet."

I was completely numb as if I were living in some alternate universe. My body was on autopilot as I walked up a wide stairway, looking for Courtroom L23. Everything was very bright, with glass "walls" and shiny, light-colored floors. At the top of the stairs were several long hallways with a multitude of numbered doors.

We found courtroom 23 at the end of such a hallway and sat on the built-in, cold, stone benches along the walls. Several people were standing by—young, old, white, Hispanic, black, children, teenagers, men, women, dressed up, dressed down, all awaiting their fate.

I could feel the somberness in the air. It was like nothing I had ever felt. As I sat there and waited, I saw my parents coming down the hallway with David. My heart skipped a beat, and for a split second, I jumped for joy as I saw my little boy. The last time we saw each other was at Orangewood.

I started walking down the hallway with open arms, ready to scoop him up. But as soon as he saw me, he ran the other way. My joy quickly turned to heartbreak. My son was running away from me. He didn't trust me. Could I blame him? First, he gets ripped away in the middle of the night, and then I leave him again at the shelter. My heart was repeatedly shattered at every one of those memories that entered my head. My little boy had lost his innocence. All in the name of what this court deemed "the best interest of the child." There was nothing I could do at that point. I stood back, giving him his space and wondering, *Will I ever have my son back?*

He ran back to my mom and clung to her leg for dear life. My mom then took him outside to stay with Tatiana while we were in court. When my mom came back, I hugged her, both of us holding back tears yet smiling at the little "secret" paper she had handed me. We waited, and waited, and waited for our name to be called. Even though I agreed to Art's plan, I walked into that courthouse thinking, *This is not going to happen. The judge and lawyers will see how absurd this is. It's going to be different for us. God is faithful.* I gripped the little piece of paper my mom handed me in my hand.

Our hearing was scheduled at 8:00 a.m., yet our name wasn't called until close to 10:00. As we waited, our attorneys pulled us aside to confirm we were all on the same page. My husband's lawyer reminded him once again to keep in mind that all "the system" cared about was the "children's best interest." Therefore, in response to any question regarding me, or in trying to defend me … don't. They both made sure to emphasize that if we didn't "play along," the system would take our children away.

Right before walking in, Art looked at me and said, "Okay, I want you to be psychologically prepared to be really mad when you read the report. They're going to lie about you. They are going to take things out of context. But don't worry about any of that right now. Just stick to the plan."

Our name was called, our lawyers stood up, and in we went. My heart was racing as I walked into that room. I was innocent. Yet the fate of my family rested with this sea of nameless faces. My family in Brazil was on their knees, praying; missionaries in Africa, on their knees, praying; friends in Switzerland, praying; all over the U.S., praying. I was pleading with God, praying that this judge would see the preposterousness of it all and close the case that day.

The hearing began. I just watched, still in shock that this was even happening, heart palpitating, as the legal formalities started. I was sitting on the left side of the courtroom. The children's court-appointed lawyer and social services' lawyers were seated to the left of me. Ricardo was sitting to my right with our lawyers. My mom and stepdad were in a sitting area behind us, along with our next-door neighbors Mike and Kathy, who offered to come as witnesses.

I don't really remember what was said in the courtroom. I just kept waiting for the judge to call my name, and it would be my turn to tell him what happened. I imagined it would be something like Judge Judy, where one side says one thing, the other side says one thing, and the judge questions them back and forth.

As a matter of fact, now that I look back, where was Dora, the social worker? Shouldn't she be being questioned? How about Officer Locker? Or the detectives Cruz and Sword? How about the nanny, Shannon? This was, in fact, a court of law, right? Apparently not so. Here I was, being judged with no proof to pinpoint me, yet they were considering taking my children away.

I glanced over at the court-appointed children's lawyer, whom I had never met. She swooshed through the papers, then slowed down while taking a closer look at the character letters. She slowly and turned each page one by one, carefully taking notes, giving me a glimmer of hope that she might say something to the judge. I kept waiting for my turn to speak and tell my side of the story.

The judge asked all parties involved if they all agreed with giving the father sole custody. He turned to me, and during the only time I ever got to speak in that courtroom, I confirmed. The judge turned to my husband, and he confirmed. He turned to the children's lawyer … confirmed. He turned to social services (SSA) … *DENIED. You have got to be kidding me!* I thought.

When asked why, the SSA lawyer stated that they did not have a chance to speak with the father prior to the hearing; therefore, they didn't know whether he was a "fit" father or not. Ricardo and I instantly turned to each other and made eye contact, both knowing what the other was thinking.

Was it any coincidence that on the fateful night when Ricardo arrived from his business trip, and the police were "interviewing" us at the hospital, they explicitly told him not to speak to the SSA agents?

At that point, the hearing was in recess while our lawyers battled it out with the judge and SSA lawyers. Art told me, "Okay, read everything in this court report and just outline what you think is incorrect/inconsistent/out of context." There were about three hundred pages. I skimmed through most of it, searching for quotation marks from anyone I had spoken to in the seventy-two hours before this hearing. I also looked for the nanny's name.

The first thing that caught my eye was Officer Locker's report stating, "Mother did not seem empathetic towards [victim] Lucas. Her attitude seemed like it was a normal hospital visit."

The sense of betrayal I had initially felt came flooding back. I had been shot from behind by these purported public servants who were there to help me. I kept picturing that hospital room. Dora and I were sitting on the pullout couch while Officer Locker casually leaned against the wall and questioned me. He didn't seem very "empathetic" either!

People were making assumptions about my character after meeting me for a couple of minutes in what was probably one of the most traumatic incidents I have ever experienced. I kept reading and found yet another little snippet, this time from the public health nurse. She stated, "Mother was observed talking with a friend and laughing as the child was having a seizure."

This was one of the statements I underlined, thinking, *What?! I never did this!* As I continued to flip through the pages, I saw Doctor Wong's assessment. She is what is known as a CAP (Child Abuse Pediatrician), although she never identified herself as such to me. She simply told me she was the pediatrician on call at the PICU.

When I saw Art for the first time at his office, he had asked me if I had spoken to this doctor. I told him I had, and he immediately raised his voice, "Do not talk to that woman! She is the devil."

I remember being shocked at his response, thinking, *How bad can she be? She's a doctor!* Well, here was her statement to the court: "I believe the baby's injury was non-accidental in nature as there is no plausible explanation for the baby's injury. The baby's injury could only be caused by blunt force trauma. It should be noted, as I walked into the child's hospital room on July 9, 2015, I found the parents on their cell phones while the child was actively seizing in bed. Parents did not alert the staff child was seizing. It is further noted the father questioned me about possible injury scenarios and requested the child's monitors be turned down, and/or off during the first night so the mother could sleep."

Was this woman really accusing me of purposefully hurting my infant son with a blunt object? *Really?!* Then she goes on with more character assassinations of my husband and me, saying we were on our phones while our son was seizing? *Yes! It was the next day when our other son was MISSING! We were on our phones calling lawyers and social workers!*

The idea that I would simply ignore my baby's seizures? We were told that Lucas was having about fifteen seizures an hour. They had him hooked up to a 24-hour EEG (electroencephalogram) monitor, and the doctors themselves were trying to figure out what type of seizure he was having and what medication would work for him.

But they expected me, a layman and a mother whose other child is missing, to know when my seven-week-old son is having a seizure? They also implied that my husband was "plotting" different scenarios and that he cared more about my health than my son's. Art was right. Reading all of this was infuriating, and the fact that I would never get to dispute any of this or defend myself made it that much more unfair. Let's just say I now understand the purpose of pleading the Fifth.

Before I could read anything else, our names were called again. The recess was over. I told Mike and Kathy to go home since it was becoming pretty obvious that no one but the lawyers would speak. We walked back in, and I watched our lawyers argue that my husband was out of state when the incident took place, so it shouldn't even be a question whether he had any involvement, regardless of whether SSA got to talk to him or not. He was not a suspect, and he had no prior history of child abuse (or any record at all, for that matter; then again, neither did I).

By the grace of God, the judge overruled SSA's objection and ruled that the children would go to their biological father. He went on to make further provisions, stating that Ricardo be put on a "CRISP-like" program (CRISP stands for Conditional Release and Intensive Supervision Program, and is only available to residents of Orange County; we were living in LA County); and I would have twenty-four hours to vacate the premises of the family home and remove all my belongings. Caseworkers would contact us with further details.

I walked out of that courtroom, bawling uncontrollably while my mom held me. Both of us were in pure disbelief. I can't help but assume both of us were asking God *"why"* at this moment, especially after having meditated on that Bible verse with such conviction. *What was God doing?*

Art stood outside the courtroom, watching us cry, and said, "I told you this is what was going to happen." But I couldn't believe it. My head said one thing; my heart felt another. I was stripped of everything I cherished—my husband, my children, my home. We sat down in the hallway and cried some more.

I remember shaking, thinking, *This has to be a bad dream ... this is not happening.* My husband and my stepfather were in shock and not very expressive at all. Our world was spinning; everything was so overwhelming. I had just signed documents agreeing that I couldn't see my children without approved monitors, all of whom had yet to be determined. I couldn't handle the thought of seeing David and not being able to hug him or hold him, not even to say goodbye. I asked my mom to go ahead of me and get David home. Crying, I texted my family and friends the news. Of course, everyone was horrified, disgusted, in disbelief, and feeling beyond helpless. All I could think of were my boys, especially David since he would remember. He was going to be so confused, scared, divided, and heartbroken.

I stayed with my husband and Art in the courthouse. I had a barrage of questions for him: "What about the nanny? When am I going to see my son? How long is this going to last? Where is the police investigation? Why wasn't anyone here? Why didn't I get to say anything? Where am I supposed to live now?"

In his usual fashion, Art stared me in the eye and said, "I can't answer any of that right now. What you need to do is go home, clear everything out, call Dr. Wrinkler, and enroll in the 53-week child abuse class and the 24-week parenting class. Schedule your individual sessions with her as well. Later, call Fred, my private investigator, and set a time with him to go over your case. While Lucas is in the hospital, you can sleep there. Don't leave *one* toothbrush behind!"

"What happens when it's time for Lucas to go home?" I asked.

"We'll have to cross that bridge when we get there."

The hearing adjourned. And with one fell swoop of a gavel, my entire life was changed forever.

8

Losing Everything

I headed home with Ricardo to get my things out of my house. It was all so surreal. My friend Aline came over to help me pack. As soon as we saw each other, we opened our arms and clung to each other, crying. "I'm so sorry Quel, I'm sorry … amiga … " is all she could say, and all I could do was cry. Every once in a while, we would pull away and look each other in the face, with pain but strength in our eyes.

"God is faithful," we'd say in Portuguese. We wiped each other's tears and got to work. I must have donated half my wardrobe and thrown out all the lotions and potions. I was left with nothing but the bare minimum.

My neighbors, Mike and Kathy, graciously offered their home to store all my belongings. They had seen me pregnant the first time, when it ended in a miscarriage. Kathy hugged me, saying, "I know how much you love these babies." Mike was in tears as he hauled my boxes to his house. He hugged me in disbelief. We had absolutely no idea when I would be allowed to move back home. I packed a few essentials and headed to my temporary abode, the hospital where Lucas remained.

My entire family and circle of friends were so affected by this. Everyone wanted to help but didn't know how to. One thing we knew *never* failed was *prayer*. I had nothing left to hold onto but my faith. I remember praying something like, "God, I don't know what is happening. I don't know why this is happening. I don't know what I'm supposed to do. Please make a way,

Lord. Please."

In less than five days, I had seemingly lost everything I loved. So many questions were racing through my mind, and every time I spoke to Art, the plot seemed to thicken. I am an only child, and my entire extended family lives in Brazil. When the court decided to kick me out of my house, I had nowhere to go. My mom was now the primary caretaker for David during the day while Ricardo worked, so they wouldn't let me live with her.

I was in survival mode, but deep down, I knew God was with me throughout this entire court ordeal. I remember calling my cousin Christina one night at the hospital where I was still sleeping. All I could do was cry as I mumbled my pain and concerns about David.

"What will my sons think of me?" I asked her.

And she said, "You stop that right now. Don't believe anything they're telling you. One day your sons are going to call you blessed and a God-fearing woman, you hear me?"

I immediately knew what passage she was referring to—Proverbs 31. My tears turned from grief to this feeling of meekness and submission. *Am I becoming that woman? The virtuous woman?* God was putting me on a mission. My aunt Didi took the phone away from Christina, and as she also began to cry, my aunt told me she met with their pastor during their weekly prayer meetings. She told me he had the entire congregation stand (five thousand-plus people) and point their hands towards the north (since they are in South America, and we are in North America) as he led the church in prayer for our family, rebuking the devil's attack in my life.

He and some members of the church decided to go on a fast from that point on for our family.

"What?! Are you serious?" I couldn't believe my ears. Having grown up in a family of pastors, I didn't always appreciate it. Now, because of my dad's and grandpa's legacies, I had thousands praying and fasting for me!

I thought, *How great is our God?* Truly, "Great is our Lord, and abundant in power; his understanding is beyond measure" (Psalm 147:5 ESV).

They weren't the only ones praying for us. The Sunday before our court date, my mom and dad went to church. Our pastor was away for work, but his wife, Sue, was there. My mom went to speak to her, not even sure if she would know who we were. When my mom asked her if she knew us, Sue replied with something like, "But of course! The beautiful couple with that gorgeous little boy ..." (referring to David). My mom nodded somberly and told her everything that had happened to Lucas. She asked if Sue could go to the hospital to pray for Lucas. It was late Tuesday night when Sue came, after the hearing had already taken place. Visiting hours were over, but Sue had a "Clergy" badge, so she was allowed in.

When she saw the state Lucas was in, she turned to me and opened her arms. She just held me, not saying a word, and I cried. I don't think I had had time to even process what had happened to my baby. I was mourning what seemed like the death of both my sons, even though they were still alive.

Once I gathered some composure, she pulled herself away from me and said she had been praying all day. "I've been praying, and God told me you are coming home with me." I was speechless! My pain suddenly turned into immense gratitude.

"Thank you," I sobbed. God had made a way. I was beginning to see what would be the lesson of a lifetime. God appointed gratitude as one of the essential guardians of our souls. To kindle a deep feeling of thankfulness is the only way to survive. In this world, we are fair game to the devil if we don't allow gratitude to guard our hearts. The presence of a struggle, the sense of injustice and pain, while at the same time having a sense of community, is exactly the way God designed us to be strengthened and encouraged in the faith.

My friends also grieved and shared my suffering, which drew us closer together. That last week in the hospital, my friends Rafael and Arami traveled for hours to come and pray for Lucas. There were people literally all over the world praying for our family. I was never alone, even if I was in an empty room. God was creating a beautiful quilt by sewing the hearts of individuals together with the threads of love. The Bible says that with love comes greater understanding: "... that their hearts may be encouraged, being knit together in love, to reach all the riches of full assurance of *understanding and the knowledge of God's mystery, which is Christ, in whom are hidden all the treasures of wisdom and knowledge*" (Colossians 2:2, emphasis added).

9

Meeting the PI

The initial hospital visit, the hearing, and the legal work were chaotic, but then things began to settle down. On my way to Sue's house from the hospital one night, I made an appointment to meet with Art's private investigator (PI), whose name was Fred. It was very late at night, and the only thing open was a Starbucks. When I had spoken with him on the phone, he told me to find a secluded area within the store to talk and not have any "looky-loos" or anybody trying to surveil us.

I walked in, picked a corner spot in the back of the store, and waited for him. I remember feeling so eerie and uneasy while waiting for Fred to arrive. Flashbacks of *Mission Impossible* or *True Crime* scenes were scrolling through my head. *What am I doing? Am I really meeting a private investigator?* Not a day went by where I wouldn't have thoughts like, *Is this really happening?*

I was expecting some kind of James Bond-looking guy. I saw this older gentleman walking toward me. He was probably in his early seventies, had white hair, and a long white beard. He saw me, walked towards me, stuck out his hand, and introduced himself.

"Rachel?" he asked.

I smiled and nodded. We shook hands. "Let's go over here, where there's less noise," he said.

I was very "weirded out," for lack of a better term, by all of this. I didn't know who to trust, what to say, what to do, or how to act. Since reading the court report where they described me as "non-empathetic," "not emotional enough," "laughing on the phone," I felt like everything I did would be used against me.

I had been living under a microscope. The investigators watched me, and every movement and word I said was recorded. People I assumed were on my side and were there to support me—because they said they were there "to help me"—ended up betraying me. How was this guy going to be any different?

Right off the bat, he did not fit the Hollywood depiction of a PI—he looked more like Santa Claus! He could probably tell how apprehensive I was and just started a conversation with me to break the ice. It turned out he went to the same graduate school I did, and we immediately hit it off. He told me about his background in the Marines and other three-letter government agencies. He was now retired in private practice doing this as a side gig.

He told me he had worked with Art for many years and said not to let Art get to me. "He has the worst bedside manner, but he's the best at what he does. The way he talks to you, multiply that tenfold in how he talks to the judges and lawyers in that courtroom defending you."

He was very diplomatic, of course, and told me, "Unfortunately, this is what they do. Listen to Art and do what he tells you. If he makes you cry, call me."

Little did I know how many times I'd be calling Fred for this very reason.

I gave Fred a play-by-play of what happened and what the court had ordered me to do. He wrote down every detail.

I asked, "Do they really think I did this? Is this really going to happen?

And he said, "Oh, yeah. They do this all the time."

I said, "But I didn't do this. Aren't they going to go after the nanny?"

He said, "They may, they may not. That's why I'm here—to see if we can find any red flags on her. See if we can find anything on her so that we can establish a case when you go to trial."

I thought, *This is just unbelievable.*

He asked me for all the information I had regarding the nanny—referrals, resume, background check, etc. I began picking his brain, wondering if Art was just exaggerating. He asked me about the nanny's husband and what was going on. What was their marriage like? Why was she doing this at night when her husband lived in San Diego and we lived in Cerritos, which is in a different county?

"She told me that he's in the Marines, he's stationed in San Diego, and she had two kids herself. She needed someone to help her with her young children, so she moved in with her mom while her husband focused on his career and training." That's all I knew about her husband. I didn't know his name, I didn't know anything about him, but I knew he was in the Marines.

Fred had access to people in the Marines. He made me feel a whole lot better about everything that night. He reassured me that he believed me. Fred gave me some "Jane Bond" homework to do, as he called it. He said, "I want you to go online. Do you have her on Facebook? Do you have her on Instagram? Do you have her on any of the social media platforms?"

I said, "I don't, but I will now."

He said, "You go in there. You find everything you can about her—her family, husband's family, brothers, sisters, aunts, uncles, cousins, coworkers. Anything you can find, jot it down and give it to me before she gets lawyered up and gets everything blocked."

I got to Sue's house pretty late that night, but I remembered I still had to pump milk for Lucas. From the beginning of my pregnancy, I had planned on exclusively breastfeeding. Even though I wouldn't be able to nurse my baby at night because of my epilepsy, I pumped all day to store a "stash" for the nighttime feedings. I had quite a bit leftover in the freezer, which I brought to the hospital while Lucas was there. Sadly, I wasn't producing enough to keep up with his demand.

I remember pumping for half an hour before bed, and two little ounces came out. My body was under immense physical and emotional stress. I didn't have that bonding experience you would normally have with your newborn child. Biologically, the touch, the feel, the smell between baby and mom makes your body produce the milk, and I saw that I couldn't do it anymore. It just wasn't working. I was stressing myself out.

Breastfeeding during this time was a major point of conflict between my husband and me. Ricardo was very adamant that I breastfeed our children, and I agreed. He kept asking me every night, "Are you doing it? Are you doing it?"

I said, "I'm trying, but I can't. My body isn't working. This isn't normal for my body. It's not normal for me to be doing this since I have no contact with my baby I'm trying to produce milk for." I don't know if it's because he's a man, but he just couldn't understand or relate. This really hurt me. I felt he was more concerned about breastfeeding than he was about me. That night at Sue's house, I decided to quit trying to pump. I remember feeling guilt and shame that I couldn't do for Lucas what I did for David. I cried, grieving that phase of my child's life, which I would never get back again. My baby was now alone in a hospital. I wasn't going to be home during the day or at night.

It felt like I was losing my child. It felt like I was grieving a death, but my son was still there. Those nights, when all I could feel was pain, I lay there in bed by myself. I couldn't sleep, couldn't read. I couldn't even pray. All I could do was cry. But there was a little voice in my head, even in my tears, that would bring up Bible verses. Bible verses I had memorized and learned as a child. I grew up hearing them but never really had the opportunity to put them into action. During those dark nights, I finally put those Bible verses to use.

As I was crying, not knowing what to pray, I remembered there was a verse somewhere in the Bible that says the Spirit intercedes even through our groans when we don't know what to pray (Romans 8:26). The Holy Spirit reminded me of that and took away the shame, and the guilt over not being able to pray. I just cried. All I did was cry. And again, as I was crying, more Bible verses came to my head, "Draw near to him. He'll draw near to you." (James 4:8). In my groaning, the Bible verses became my prayer. I said, "God, please come near to me. I have no one. I have nothing. I feel alone. Please come to me."

And He did come to me. He hugged me, hugged my soul like a dad putting his hand on my head and just telling me, *It's okay. Cry. Let it all out. I'm here for you. Nothing you're going through is going to be in vain, Rachel. I see you.*

Trust Me. I have your kids in My hand. Your husband is in my hand. Your home is in my hand. Be still.

And just like a little child falls asleep when Mom or Dad is reading them their bedtime stories, that became my relationship with God every night while I was at Sue's house.

10

New Normal

B y this time, I had been assigned a caseworker, and she had granted me seven hours a week of monitored visitation with both of my sons. I had also started the court-ordered "services" like Art had told me: child abuse, parenting, and individual counseling. The following day I would have a court-ordered visit with David at the county's visitation center. It would be under the supervision of a social worker since my monitors had not yet been vetted or approved. The last time David had seen me was the short encounter at the courthouse, and before that, at the Orangewood nightmare. This supervised visit was approximately one week later. I didn't know what to feel as I pulled up into the parking lot of the same place where my heart had been completely shattered.

Knowing I was now being watched—and that anything I did or said would wind up in a court report a la Dr. Wong—made me very anxious. I checked in with the receptionist and waited in a room of broken hearts. Some children were playing around. Women, men, and some teenagers with somber faces seemingly stared into space.

A woman opened the door and called my name. I got up, and she introduced herself as Elizabeth, the social worker who would be supervising my visit that day. She took me into a room filled with toddler toys, and my heart just broke into a million different pieces again as I saw David. He must have been so confused, but I couldn't say anything. I was always watched, scrutinized. He was acting out, disobeying me like he'd lost all respect and trust.

Elizabeth, fortunately, seemed to understand the situation. She told me it was okay to "discipline" him if he was doing something to "put his life in danger," like sticking his fingers into the electrical outlets. I asked her if we could go outside since he seemed very disinterested in the toys. It was my regular practice to take him outside during the day and walk around our neighborhood. There was a school near our house, and the kids loved seeing "the baby" on the sidewalk while they were at recess.

All the routines and playtimes I had with David would never be the same. She agreed to go outside with me, where there was a grass area for him to play. There I began seeing my "real" David, running, jumping, curiously looking around. He would hand me things and ask what they were. It almost felt normal again.

After observing our interaction for about an hour, Elizabeth told me we had to "wrap things up" as I was only given seven hours a week of visitation. Flashbacks of Orangewood started coming to me, my heart beating through my chest. *How am I going to say goodbye to him again?* She told me I could choose my own monitors and give her their information so she could vet them. All I could think was, *I have to say goodbye to David once again.*

I kneeled on the floor and hugged him. I told him I would see him again tomorrow. I tried my very darnedest not to cry, expecting the same outcome we had before, where the social worker essentially tore him away from me. But this time, it was different. This time, he didn't cry. It was like he realized this was just the way things were going to be. I don't know which time hurt more. Of course, I would never want to see my son in pain or suffering like he did that day in Orangewood, but at the same time, his expressing pain let me know there was still some attachment to me. Now it was like he had become detached. *Would I ever regain my baby's trust? Did he still love me?*

It felt like I had lost him forever. I wanted to scream, *"I'm sorry they did this to you, David! I'm sorry Mommy couldn't protect you! I'm sorry! I'm sorry! I'm sorry!"*

I waved goodbye one last time and turned around, not looking back while the tears streamed down my face. I got in my car and sobbed. *This can't be happening ... when is this nightmare going to end? Someone, please wake me up. Why is this happening? What is the purpose of this?*

I turned on the car and headed to my first individual counseling appointment that day. I had no idea what to expect. Everything was still very raw, and I was anxious about speaking with anyone associated with "the system," as Art had made me very aware.

My counselor's name was Dr. Wrinkler. She was an older woman, very experienced in this line of work with social services. She asked me what had brought me to her office. As soon as I mentioned CPS (child protective services) and Art, she nodded her head and said, "I'm sorry," as if this wasn't the first time. She didn't even ask or suspect me of harming my children; she just knew this was the modus operandi of CPS.

"So, how are you holding up?" she asked me.

I replied, "As best as I can, considering the circumstances." My words and how they could be spun were always in the back of my mind, so I chose my answer very carefully. I shared with her that I had just seen my son David at the visitation center, and I couldn't hold back my tears.

"How can they do this to him?" I wept. "What is my son going to think?" She just nodded and affirmed my feelings.

"At this point, I don't know what's worse," I said. "Seeing him for an hour a day or not seeing him at all! It's like having a band-aid ripped off a fresh wound every time we see each other. This can't be good for him! It's traumatizing him more!"

Again, she just nodded. Based on what the court reports said about me not being emotional enough or not empathetic towards my son, this was probably a good outburst to have. Dr. Wrinkler would also be writing court reports.

She then asked me, "Aside from the pain, which is understandable, how are you feeling about yourself? Your identity? Here you are, a mother, a wife, and they are accusing you of being a criminal. How has this affected your identity?"

I took a moment and really thought about the question. "Hmmm ... It hasn't, really."

"How so?" she asked.

"Yes, I'm a mother," I said. "Yes, I'm a wife. But first and foremost, I'm the daughter of (I pointed my finger up to the ceiling) ... the Most High. No one can take that away from me."

She seemed perplexed by my response, and after a few seconds of delayed reaction, she said, "That's a good way to look at it."

This moment marked the beginning of when I began to have of an acute awareness of the Holy Spirit. Later that day, I kept thinking, *Did I really say that? Wow ...*

But it was the truth. My entire Christian upbringing was coming out of me—something I never valued growing up. I had assumed everyone had the same upbringing as I did and memorized all the Bible verses, etc. The verse in Proverbs came to mind, "Train up a child in the way he should go; even when he is old he will not depart from it" (Proverbs 22:16 ESV), which my mom was always very faithful to do, whether I liked it or not.

After my counseling session, I went to the hospital to see Lucas and figure out a visitation schedule for David. I was flooded with friends who offered to be monitors. The logistics, however, were so complicated. Lucas was in a hospital in one county; I was now not allowed to go home where David was in another county. My mom couldn't be a monitor because she was the primary caregiver during the day while Ricardo worked—it was a challenge, to say the least.

Not to mention that my husband now had to run a business while soon taking care of a newborn who just had brain surgery and a very traumatized toddler. We had no idea how we were going to do this. We again turned to prayer and waited.

Everything was happening so fast. I was on an emotional roller coaster—happiness and relief for my sons, while at the same time sadness and pain because I couldn't be with them. I had to remind myself to listen to that subtle voice in my inner being, "Be still, and know that I am God" (Psalm 46:10).

I had been sleeping at Sue's house for days now, and every morning I would head to the hospital to spend the day with Lucas. While driving one morning, I realized that the same song was always playing on my iPod in the car–"Knowing You (All I Once Held Dear)" by Joseph Garlington. I picked it up to see if it was set on repeat. It wasn't, so I just let it be. This time, I paid attention to the song as I drove to the hospital.

I began to cry when I heard the first verse. Like a punch in the gut it reminded me of a Bible verse: "Do not love the world or the things in the world. If anyone loves the world, the love of the Father is not in him" (2 John 2:15). What I was experiencing, the loss of my family (however temporary), felt like I had lost everything. The verse reminded me of the very beginning of my motherhood journey where I was struggling to meet the world's expectations of me, not God's.

The song went on and another familiar verse popped in my head: "Then I considered all that my hands had done and the toil I had expended in doing it, and behold, all was vanity and a striving after wind, and there was nothing to be gained under the sun" (Ecclesiastes 2:11). Those expensive pieces of paper on the wall—my diplomas. Something I had spent countless hours to earn—reading, researching, studying. Starting a business from scratch with my husband—hours of putting presentations together, market research, thousands spent on physical tools. And here I was at the fate of a judicial system that cared nothing about whether I had a higher education or not.

By the third verse it hit me. This is the purpose. There is nothing more valuable in this world than having a relationship with Jesus, just as it says in the Bible: "But whatever gain I had, I counted as loss for the sake of Christ. Indeed, I count everything as loss because of the surpassing worth of knowing Christ Jesus my Lord" (Philippians 3:7-8). How did I forget this? I had been bombarded with so much bad news. In a short time, I experienced so much trauma. The devil was using every trick in his book to get me to take my eyes off Jesus. I can't express in words what an awakening I experienced with this song. This is what every Christian has been taught, but have they experienced it? God reminded Paul in 2 Corinthians 12:9 that His grace is enough. But is it, though? Then this song. It is. It was. It always will be—God's grace is enough.

I was living this song. "They" had taken everything away from me. My house. My business. My family. But I still had Jesus. All I had was Jesus. And that was enough. This was the purpose. I was getting to *know Jesus* like I had never known Him before. My tears of pain and hurt became tears of joy, the lyrics reminding me of everything I had been taught about my identity and purpose as a "child of god" (1 John 3:1).

"Thank You, Jesus, for always being by my side. Whatever happens, Your will be done, Lord. If the Son of Man suffered (Mark 8:31), then who am I to *not* suffer?" I cried some more. The song then changes keys from a soft melody into a *crescendo* tune of victory. Reminding the listener that in our suffering we become like Jesus, and He is our deliverer, our redeemer, our hope is this broken world. To this day I can't listen to this song without crying. I pondered this song all day long as I held Lucas, and just poured my heart and soul into his, grateful for everything that had passed. Drawing closer and closer to God with every breath from that day forward.

11

Lucas Goes Home

Every week, I had my routine: Wake up in the morning, go to the hospital to see Lucas, spend a few hours there, go to one of my classes. After that, I'd usually have my visitation with David. Then I'd go back home and do some homework I was still working on with Fred. So the days went by. Lucas had been in the PICU for about eleven days, and he was finally being moved into a regular hospital room since he wasn't needing the constant monitoring anymore.

Now the goal was to teach him how to feed from the bottle. Lucas would be heading home soon to my husband, who would have to handle single parenthood while I still couldn't go home and take care of my boys. Everything lay in a balance. If we couldn't find a way to prove to social services that we could adequately provide care for our sons, then the entire case could go up in flames. They wouldn't let my mom take care of my children either because she was with my son when he was seized. Therefore she was now part of the investigation.

The doctors who were following all of Lucas's progress felt he was stable and healthy enough to go home on July 20, 2015. But social services had other plans. Before Lucas was officially discharged to go home to be with his father, and before I was able to move back home, they demanded a series of exams. Medical exams that were really unnecessary, even in the eyes of his pediatrician. One of those exams was another skeletal survey. Lucas was seven weeks old when his injury happened. During that initial ER trip, he had already had the CT scan and the skeletal survey.

On July 17, I received a phone call from my family in Brazil. My family had been very involved with everything, and they knew we were struggling to find care for our sons once Lucas was discharged from the hospital. My aunt Didi, cousin Priscila, and mother-in-law Rita had a plan. I had lived in the USA for nearly thirty years, and my aunt Didi had never come to visit me out of fear of flying. But now, when push came to shove, she, along with my cousin Priscila, decided to drop everything and come take care of my boys. My mother-in-law paid for their plane tickets.

Once again, God had perfect timing. I remember hearing the news and us just crying on the phone together. I couldn't thank them enough! Priscila (a dentist) left her full-time dental practice to come to take care of my babies. My mother-in-law, who couldn't come herself, offered her hard-earned money to my family. And my aunt Didi, my dad's sister, forgot her fear and instead focused on her love for me.

Things seemed to be aligning and moving in the right direction. Lucas was still in the hospital but improving exponentially every day. He was no longer on assisted breathing, received no medical sedation, and was out of the PICU! He was a true miracle. A living testament of God's love, mercy, power, and grace. We were informed he would soon be going home, which was bittersweet news to me. I had unlimited access to him while he was in the hospital, but everything was about to change once again.

While waiting for my cousin and aunt to be vetted and approved as monitors, I had my friend Tatianna monitor visits for me. She worked full-time and graciously offered to visit on her lunch break. I met her at the mall, where David got dropped off by my mom, and we began this very awkward, forced visit, knowing we were on a timer.

I really couldn't have any quality time with David, as he was so distracted by everything at the mall. I felt like a babysitter or a playmate to my son. It seemed to be only a matter of seconds before our time was up. Tatianna would go with me to my mom's car, where I would say goodbye. David was thrilled to see my mom (his grandma) but didn't really seem to care about me. Tatianna, knowing me, would start crying even before I did. We walked back to the mall, she hugged me, and we cried. "I'm so sorry, Quel ... " (pronounced Kel, my nickname in Portuguese). "What's going to happen to that *vaca*?!" (cow in Portuguese) referring to the nanny. I shrugged my shoulders. "I don't know."

The day we had all been praying for finally came. After twelve days in the hospital, Lucas was officially headed home following brain surgery. He was nothing short of a miracle. God was in that surgery room guiding the doctors' hands. As I waited for Ricardo to pick him up, I pondered the last two weeks and everything that had happened.

I remembered Officer Locker questioned me that infamous night, asking why I had brought Lucas to this particular hospital (being that I lived in another county). I thanked God in that moment that I had. I discovered through paperwork and speaking with hospital staff that the only two pediatric neurosurgeons in all of LA and Orange County were in that hospital the day I took Lucas in. He probably would not have survived had I called 911 and been taken to the nearest hospital. God knows!

Lucas was sent home that day with no concerning signs of brain damage. He was on anti-convulsant medication following a series of seizures after surgery due to the irritation the blood had caused his brain. He was heading home to be with his dad and his big brother. My aunt Didi and cousin Priscila were already home waiting for them.

I was still processing the fact that I would no longer be able to be with Lucas all day, as I had been while he was in the hospital. I can't describe the pain because there are no words. I had carried him for nine months in my belly, and in such a short time, he was ripped away from me.

The bonding that occurs in those first three months, the nursing, the cuddling, the skin-to-skin contact ... I would never be able to get back. We had both been robbed. I felt like I was just a temporary holding place for one hour a day. I honestly don't remember how I said goodbye to him at the hospital. My brain must have blocked out this trauma. I do remember going to CAT (Child Abuse Treatment) that week and everyone celebrating that Lucas had left the hospital and was home with his dad. At the same time, the moms in there could see the tears in my eyes. They understood my grief and my pain, and they cried with me. It was a very dystopian support group.

Sometime following the week Lucas went home, I had an appointment to take a psychiatric evaluation. Just another preemptive measure Art had me do in preparation for trial. I remember Fred warning me to be careful what I told this psychiatrist, as he would possibly testify when the trial came. I had no idea what a "psych eval" was, but most of my fellow CAT classmates knew. They had already been through it, and they told me it was brutal.

The standard test is the MMPI (Minnesota Multiphasic Personality Inventory), consisting of 567 true/false questions, plus eight essay questions. It took me two days and a total of eight hours to complete.

I remember driving to this doctor's office about one hour away from where I lived. It was hot that day. I walked toward the receptionist's desk, told her I was there for a psychiatric evaluation, and handed her a check for $310. She took me to the back room where there were a bunch of desks, like in school, with wood partitions between each person so they couldn't "cheat."

She handed me a huge, spiral-bound book with a blank answer sheet and told me, "You are to answer all the questions truthfully with regard to how you feel at the present moment."

I sat down and began this monstrous task. As I read through, I noticed it kept asking the same questions over and over, just worded differently. A certain paranoia wanted to kick in as I started getting in my own head, *What are they really trying to get at with these questions?*

Certain true/false statements stood out to me, like, "I sometimes feel like I am being watched." *Well, duh! Yes! I am! Living under a microscope!* I thought. Or statements like this: "Sometimes I feel people are against me." Another eye roll moment, *Yes! The entire system is against me!*

There were other obvious statements, such as, "I feel anxious" or "I feel depressed." And it was 567 questions! I couldn't finish it all in one sitting. After roughly five hours, I was brain dead, and I had a visit with David one hour away. I asked the receptionist if I could come back the next day to finish, and she agreed. I don't even remember my visit with David; I was so exhausted from everything.

I went home to Sue's house that night and read a devotional from a book she gave me called "Jesus Calling" by Sarah Young. "Bring me all your feelings, even the ones you wish you didn't have. Fear and anxiety still plague you … these attacks from the evil one come at you relentlessly. Use your *shield of faith to extinguish those flaming arrows* . . . Do not hide your fear or pretend it isn't there … Bring your anxieties out into the Light of My Presence, where we can deal with them together" (Ephesians 6:16 ESV).

This little study reminded me once again of what the Holy Spirit had been telling me the whole time. Some nights, all I could do was cry when "speaking" to God or praying. It made me feel guilty, and this little voice in my head kept saying, *Get over it, Rachel! Haven't you seen that other people's situations are so much worse than yours?* That day, I knew that it was the voice of the accuser, the devil. This nugget of Scripture showed me I didn't have to pretend with God. He knew what I was feeling, and I didn't have to be ashamed. Repeatedly acknowledging this promise slowly began healing me. It began the growth I would need to keep going for whatever length of time was ahead. I had to start living in faith rather than fear of God.

The next day, I woke up and headed back to the psychiatrist's office to complete my evaluation. Upon completion, I had a consultation with the doctor. I anxiously awaited him, remembering what Fred had told me. He introduced himself and asked me what brought me to his office. I told him it was due to a CPS investigation, and he asked me to tell him what happened the morning of July 8, 2015.

I began by telling him about the scream I heard at 4 a.m. while my son was with the nanny in the other room, then the hospital, and so on.

He responded with, "Well, that's nonsensical. It's obvious it was the nanny. Why would they think you did this?"

I tried not to grin but gave a grimace with a shoulder shrug and replied, "Yeah, I don't know."

He continued with the consultation, inquiring about my family abroad, finances, marriage, education, etc. All in all, it was a pretty short consultation, and I breathed a sigh of relief as I walked out of that office. He knew it wasn't me! This had to help my case!

Within a couple of days, the results arrived in the mail. I opened that envelope like it was Christmas day, and I was receiving my dream gift from Santa Claus. It was a lengthy evaluation—eight pages of single-spaced analysis! Oddly enough, it was quite intriguing to "learn" about myself from a psychiatric perspective. I giggled a few times while reading it, thinking, *Yeah, that's me!*

The most important part was the doctor's conclusion, of course, which stated, "The results of the psychological testing for Mrs. Bruno are consistent with an individual likely to be emotionally healthy and psychologically resilient. Therefore, she is likely able to manage a considerable degree of stress and is quite unlikely to resort to any physical abuse to a child or even to be aggressive with those around her. It is this examiner's opinion that Mrs. Bruno can very definitively benefit from reunification services."

Thank You, Jesus! I thought. At times during this process, I couldn't help but think I was going crazy. Now I tease people that I am not crazy, and I have proof! Most of the time, I thought I was going crazy for reasons you might not think. I remember asking Sue one night, "Why am I *not* going crazy? Why am I not hysterical? Is this normal? Have I become detached?"

She would assure me that the very fact I was asking if I was crazy was a sure sign that I was not crazy. When I look back on this situation, it would be completely understandable for me to lose my mind, considering everything I had been through in such a short time. Today, I know it was nothing but the grace of God that kept me sane. As I look back on that time, it was almost like an out-of-body experience, as if I were on the outside looking at this movie occurring right in front of me. But I had my eyes on hope, my eternal hope in Christ Jesus, who does not break His promises.

12

Life Under a Microscope

My life was now unrecognizable to me, while Ricardo had his own challenges. Yes, he got to go home and be with David, but as part of CRISP (Conditional Release and Intensive Supervision Program), that the judge had ordered, a social worker visited our house *three times a week*. Every other evening, basically, a stranger came to our home and observed every nitty-gritty detail—going through our pantry, looking under the kitchen and bathroom sinks, checking our refrigerator, seeing if the sheets were clean, just to name a few—and wrote it all down for the next court hearing. Before going to bed, I would always call Ricardo to check on him and David. It was never good news. David had completely changed after his return from Orangewood. He was aggressive. He was angry. He was traumatized. His whole world had been turned upside down.

We were all living on pins and needles. It seemed like at any time, for any reason, they could decide to change the arrangement as they pleased. Ricardo and I were living in two parallel universes, each experiencing their own pain—so much so that we couldn't really see each other's pain. To make matters worse, my caseworker would tell me one thing, and the social worker making the house visits would tell him another thing, creating further division and discord between us.

We would meet every night for dinner, but all we could talk about were the legal woes we faced and the psychological toll our son was paying. We failed to notice the neglect our marriage was experiencing. Maybe because I was isolated, I had no choice but to draw near to God. I had nothing else to hold onto.

I remember forgiving the nanny from the very first day. Ricardo was, understandably, furious and not so quick to forgive. All he could talk about at dinner were the police reports, when were would see the results of the investigation, and what was going to happen to the nanny. I forgave her very early on—I had to in order to maintain my communion with God. I also knew what they had done to our children, and I wouldn't wish our fate on anyone ... including the nanny.

I didn't want to focus so much on vindication; I wanted to focus on my boys. I wanted to hear how they were doing. I wanted to see pictures of them. I wanted my husband to hug me and tell me they were okay. I wanted him to ask me how I was doing, not ask me how much milk I was able to pump for Lucas. Yet he wanted to fix things; he wanted the routine to go back to normal at home. He would tell me how much David was acting out and wouldn't go to bed like usual.

I would look at him and say, "Of course not! Things are not normal, Ricardo!" He would take issue with the fact that before all of this, we had worked together as parents to establish a nighttime routine, and David was "sleep trained" at that point, but now he needed to be rocked to sleep or be in bed with my aunt or cousin. I emotionally shut down at that point and pondered in my mind, *Do you want to trade!? I'll go home and sleep with them! You can be forced to have monitored visits and child abuse classes and criminal investigations!*

That date night did not end on a happy note. I went home feeling bitter and resentful toward my husband. I also felt guilty about my feelings when I first became a mom.

Ricardo and I were living our best lives then. I had graduated and received my MBA degree, we started our own business, everything was going according to plan. Then we decided to start a family. My whole adult life, I had heard, "You can have it all. You don't have to choose between career and family." While it may work for some, that statement wasn't true for me. I was having a tough time juggling everything and feeling tremendous pressure to make my MBA "worth it." At that time, I perceived motherhood as taking me away from my career.

Now here I was, wanting nothing more than to be a mother to my two sons. I couldn't care less about my career. I had a conversation with God that night. "Why did I even bother getting those expensive pieces of paper (my diplomas) on the wall? I'm never going to use them. Especially now."

I felt a tugging in my heart, that little voice again, from the Spirit. *In due time you will use your talents. Right now, I have placed right where you need to be. Do you not see how they need you? I chose you, Rachel, to be their mom. To be Ricardo's wife.*

My heart was broken and convicted at that moment. I felt ashamed. I prayed, "Forgive me, Father. There's no greater gift or greater calling I've ever had than to serve the family you have given me. Help me remember, Lord. Create in me a clean heart, and renew the right spirit within me in Jesus' name, Amen."

I woke up the next morning and headed over to the child abuse and parenting classes (CAT, which stands for Child Abuse Treatment, and PAT, which stands for Parents As Teachers). The court had ordered me to enroll in a 53-week CAT class, a 24-week PAT class, and individual counseling. My parenting class was on Sunday mornings, meaning I couldn't go to church. Then again, it wouldn't have made much difference.

I asked social services if I could attend church with my family, being that my "monitors" were there (Priscila and aunt Didi), and it was at a public place, I figured, *Why not?*

Their response to me was that visitation was not meant to be "a family reunion." It was a time my children exclusively spent with me so my parenting skills could be observed. Once again, this agency isolated me and took away any sense of community I may have had.

Isn't that the definition of an abusive relationship? Anyway, I digress.

My life now revolved around these classes, court dates, hospital/doctor visits, and visitation schedules. When I went to my first CAT class I had no idea what to expect. I was scared, as in my mind I pictured … men?

Pedophiles? Sexual abusers? Drug addicts? Alcoholics? Gang members? This was an *abuse* class, after all.

But nothing could be further from the truth. Chairs were arranged in a circle. The class was pretty much 50/50 gender-wise, all races, all ages, with one facilitator. It was customary for the new person to tell their story. So I introduced myself and began explaining my case.

I was shocked when I saw them nodding their heads and mumbling things like, "See? Dr. Wong!" or "Yep! That's what happened to you!" while pointing at someone else in the circle. They would finish my sentences! *What?* I thought, *This happens regularly?* Apparently so. I heard so many horror stories that mine looked like a fairy tale. Art had been right all along (imagine that!). People were sent to jail. Children were separated from their siblings and moved from home to home with no reunification or visitation provided for *months.*

I couldn't reconcile what I witnessed with what I had been told my whole life. *Wait a minute, this is child protective services ... Why are they removing children from perfectly fine homes? Because of accidents at the park? Disgruntled exes ... Adoption? Foster care? I thought those were good things.*

From the moment I encountered Officer Locker and Dora, the social worker, I assumed that I had just gotten some very incompetent social workers/judges/doctors/etc. Yet these stories were proving me wrong. I was getting a whole new education here, and it had nothing to do with child abuse. Families were being targeted, tax dollars were being spent, all under the guise of "the best interest of the child."

Usually, in the mornings, I would update Sue on everything that was going on. We would laugh, cry, pray ... repeat. One morning, someone very close to me called and told me, "Rachel, I've been praying ... and one word keeps coming to my mind: Repent."

My expression must have changed because I saw Sue's expression change.

I responded back, "Okay," and hung up.

I didn't really know what to make of it. *Repent from what?*

Sue looked at me and asked, "Is everything okay?" probably thinking it was related to Lucas's health or something from the legal system.

I said, "Yeah ... this person just told me to repent."

She put her hands on her face, and said, "Oh, I'm sorry, honey. Some people ... just ... don't understand." She gave me a hug, and as she left for work, she said something to the effect of, "Just pray ... ask God that the truth be revealed."

Later that night, I remember praying about this. It prompted me to have another major shift while in communion with God. I knew the person who told me this was well-intentioned and didn't mean to hurt me. I remembered the story of Job in the Bible. His friends had told him that he must have done something to deserve everything that was happening to him.

While shuffling through Job, I remembered there was a parable in the Bible about a man who was born blind. I went looking for it and found it in John 9.

"Okay, God, who sinned? Me? My husband?" And interestingly enough, I heard an answer similar to what Jesus said to His disciples, but He also talked about a demonic strategy against the family unit. The words I felt in my core speaking to my soul: *Nothing, My child. No one has sinned. This is simply the fallen world you live in. What you are witnessing right now is about the destruction of the family. It is what the devil has been trying to do from the moment I created the family. Husband against wife, brother against brother.*

Now, I've never been one to say I have spiritual revelations, dreams, or visions, and I would never attempt to classify myself as some sort of prophet. But I can say I distinctly felt the Spirit that night, in my core, as He had been showing Himself to me from the first night at the hospital.

I began remembering my childhood Bible stories, Cain and Abel, Adam and Eve . . . everything began to click in my head. The Spirit continued, *What your family is experiencing right now will not be in vain. I will use your family; I will use your story to restore other families. Do not be afraid. Victory is yours.*

I remembered my child abuse class from earlier that day, and everyone's stories flashed before me. When Sue told me to pray that the truth be revealed, my initial thought was about Lucas's injury and the nanny. But now God was showing me the truth in my prayer—the truth about these families, about corruption, and about His purpose in all of this.

My friend Rhianna came to mind specifically. Both our sons were infants, both had bone fractures. We had the same attorney, the same caseworker, the same judge. And were both pawns in Dr. Wong's world. Rhianna had all four of her children removed and placed with strangers. Her youngest was taken from the hospital while she was at a hearing. She returned to an empty hospital bassinet, not knowing where her son had been placed.

My sorrow then turned to greater sorrow. *It's not just my family, I thought, but so much injustice all these families are suffering. So much injustice, God. Why?* My perspective shifted from focusing only on my situation to all the other families going through this without the resources or family support I had. Without knowing Jesus.

13

Homeless

About two weeks went by, and there was still no end in sight. My cousin and aunt had been living at my house and were my monitors during visits with Lucas and David. I remember one particular visit with David at the park with my cousin. By now, this was the new normal for David. He was happy to see me, would hug me and call me to play, and while I acted like this was normal, inside, I was aching.

My heart was captive to the calling of the Holy Spirit, both with joy and with tears. I was learning I could have both at the same time. My heart was heavy, longing to be reunited with my family. Yet my heart was joyful that my children were with my aunt, who loved me like a daughter, and my cousin, who was always a sister to me.

How blessed was I to have family who loved me so that they were willing to travel around the world and come to my aid? I remembered the prayer in the hospital the first night. He is mine. Everything we have on this earth belongs to God. For the first time in a long time, David cried when I put him in the car seat. I hugged him and said with confidence, "Mommy will see you again tomorrow, okay? I love you. We will see each other again soon."

Sometimes the Spirit wants us to do or say something, or to wait. With my heart held captive, immense spiritual growth happened. I trusted Jesus and obeyed. The same peace I had felt at the hospital, I felt as David drove off with my cousin. I will see him again. At this point, my stay with Sue was coming to an end. When this all started, we had no idea how long it would take, but we assumed once evidence was brought forth, the police report came out, or the social workers saw there was no abuse in our family, the case would end. That was not the case.

My pastor was returning from his trip and coming back for a family reunion they had planned months earlier. Sue told me there wouldn't be any spare bedrooms in their home, as everyone was gathering there. We had been praying that all of this would have been over by now. Unfortunately, it was not over, and it didn't look like it would be anytime soon. Of course, I understood and had to quickly figure out where I would go next.

"Homeless" again. My lawyer strongly advised me against requesting to live with my mom since she was one of the primary caretakers. He warned that social services would use this as a motive to say the family was not cooperating and were "putting the children at risk" or putting my needs above the children's.

I discussed this with Ricardo, and we concluded that it was best to find a hotel. Mind you, this was in July, the peak of summer, with limited availability everywhere and very expensive. My husband found a place close by our home, but I knew this would be financially unsustainable for us.

Lucas was almost three months old. He was taken from me shortly before his two-month milestone, and I felt like I had missed half my son's life. One hour a day was nothing. I wanted us to know each other well. Due to the trauma, I don't really have any memories that stand out to me during these visits. It was too painful to hold my baby and then give him back.

I remember one visit early on, where I met with a social worker at the mall. She observed me during a one-on-one visit with Lucas, just as they had done with David. We sat in the open spaces of the mall on a weekend in the summer, surrounded by people. I was trying to nurse Lucas while the social worker spoke to me. This was the same social worker who had been assigned to visit our home three times a week, not the one who had observed me with David.

She asked me about postpartum depression. I specifically remembered Art telling me to not talk about this. I told her I did not have postpartum depression and that I just wanted to be with my baby. Later in a court report, this particular social worker was very kind in her description of me. Then she was removed from our case with no explanation.

I was so thankful that my cousin and my aunt were my monitors. I would see Lucas and David for an hour each. It had to be in a public place. It couldn't be in anybody's home. It was peak summer and nearly 100 degrees outside, but I had to meet him in a park, at the mall, in a library.

My cousin was there with me. She was supposed to keep a little journal, writing down the interactions and sending it to the caseworker. I also kept everything documented about where I was going every week. I had to send my caseworker a schedule of my activities.

For one of the visitations with David specifically, I remember going to the park with him and my cousin. Again, my cousin and my aunt are from Brazil, so they spoke Portuguese with David at home. My husband spoke Portuguese—everybody communicating in Portuguese. But I had court documents stating I could only talk with him in English since I was still under monitored visits.

During one visit at the park, he began singing a little song that I had never heard. He looked at my cousin, and they started cheerfully singing together. Time seemed to stop at that moment for me. I was living what I had feared from the beginning. Milestones and memories that I was supposed to have with my children were happening with someone else. I wanted to cry right then and there, but the Spirit moved me. You will be together again. This will be a moment in time. I will restore.

I asked my cousin, "What is this?"

She said, "Oh, it's a DVD we brought from Brazil that we watched with him, and he's singing the song from one of the videos." And just like with the hot dog situation at Orangewood where I'd never given my son a hot dog, here again was my son reaching these milestones. He was speaking new words in Portuguese—things I didn't teach him, things I'd never seen him do. It was just painful. Painful to live, painful to accept that I would never get this time and these milestones back again.

I tried to keep those thoughts away while I was visiting my son since that was one of the only times I would get with him during the week. I would try to play with him and hug him, and at the end of the one hour, I would put him in the car. The goodbyes were always accompanied by his tears. He never wanted me to strap him in the car seat, and I would try to hold back my tears as I told him, "I will see you again. Okay? Mommy will see you again tomorrow. Okay? It's okay. You're going to go home with Didi. You're going to go home to Daddy. It's okay." Then I would give my cousin and my aunt a hug; it was a scenario covered in tears every time.

They went home. I went to the hotel room by myself and tried to get my mind off of things. I would look at the legal documents and the upcoming court hearings. I would call Fred to see if there were any updates.

The last I talked to him, Fred told me to get all the information I could and make up a timeline of all the people involved, and he was going to do the things on his side. When I called him that day, he said, "Yeah, well, I found the nanny's husband. His name is—Brandon—and he *is* in the Marines, but he is also in the police academy."

Fred asked me, "Did the nanny ever tell you that he was in the police?"

I told him, "No."

Fred said, "Yeah, this is code blue. They're not going to go after her."

It still didn't register with me. I said, "What are you talking about? They won't even interview her?"

Apparently, she was sort of a protected class under an unspoken code for police. Fred kept repeating, "They're not going to go after her." *Wow,* I remember thinking, *Really? I'm facing the possibility of going to jail and being blamed for this while she gets a pass?* Wow. I felt betrayed yet again.

He also found a protective order issued on her behalf, indicating some domestic woes in their marriage, and they were not living together. Then things started to click. She was probably looking for a way out of this marriage and trying to find a way to financially support herself.

I remembered that Fred told me to dig into the nanny's social media accounts from the very beginning. Now that I had his name, I found her husband's profile, along with that of his brother, who was also a police officer in another county nearby. His parents were divorced. Both brothers seemed very proud of their professions. The nanny had many picture-perfect family moments with her children and her husband. Looks can be very deceiving.

While none of these findings were "red flags" or incriminating, they did show me this person's character. She was very good at faking her happiness (I later found out she and her husband divorced shortly after Lucas' injury). Unfortunately, there are no tests for character in this life. Only God knows a person's heart.

Fred decided set up an undercover stealth operation with the aid of a hidden camera. He worked with his wife, who was in the private surveillance industry. She called the nanny, saying she would like to schedule an interview because she was looking for a nanny. This was well after the incident, after law enforcement and social services had already contacted the nanny. Yet she still scheduled the time, the place, and the date to meet with Fred's wife, whom the nanny thought was pregnant and looking for a nanny. His wife was going to have a friend put on a fake belly and see what she could get out of the nanny. Things had taken a fascinating turn.

The nanny's husband, Brandon, had a brother who was a police officer in a neighboring county from where this entire case happened. I began connecting the dots with a conversation I had had with a dear friend while I was getting all the character letters. She called me one night and said, "Hi, Rachel. I wrote the character letter. I just got off the phone with your caseworker and told him about you and that you were a great person. He started to ask me about the nanny. 'How much did Rachel pay her? Where did Rachel find her?' he asked me. And I just kept saying, 'I don't know. You have to ask Rachel.'"

I interrupted my friend, "Wait a minute, you said he?"

She said, "Yeah. Your caseworker. He said he was your caseworker."

I said, "No. My caseworker is a woman. Do you have the phone number or the name?"

She said, "No. He didn't tell me, and it came from a blocked phone number."

I told Fred this, and he said, "Oh, might have been his brother or somebody else within the department trying to get information since it was from a private number."

All these little clues were coming together, and I was feeling hopeful. That hope quickly dissipated when Fred told me the nanny canceled their appointment and must have lawyered up. She wouldn't return his phone calls any longer. Art was constantly reminding me, "You do not tell anybody one word about what we are doing. Okay? If these people find out that we're preparing for this, you have no idea how vengeful they are. You do not talk to these people."

I said, "They're nice."

"They are not your friends. Nobody here is your friend. The only friend you have here is me, and that's only because you paid me."

I said, "Okay, okay."

I was still living in the hotel. And after a week or so, we were running out of money. I told Art, "I can't afford this. I can't live in a hotel until this thing is over. When is this going to be over? If you could at least give me a timeline …"

"I can't give you a timeline. I don't know when this is going to be over."

"Well, I can't stay in a hotel. I can't afford it. I'm going to have to go move in with my mom or something."

He said, "You can ask the caseworker whatever you want, but I'm warning you. She's probably going to say no. She's probably going to say you're putting your children's lives at risk."

Art's reasoning was valid since my mom was still considered the primary caretaker, even though my aunt Didi and cousin Priscila were taking care of my kids at home with Ricardo. But the Court wasn't too worried about updating or including any information which might benefit me. The only caveat was I knew that if I lived with my mom, then my two sons would not be able to go to her house any longer.

I asked my mom if I could live with her and if she could accept the terms that the boys would no longer be able to go to her house if I lived there.

My mom said, "Of course."

I wrote an email to my caseworker and explained the situation. I prayed before I sent that email, "God, You know the circumstances. You know what's going on. Please, God, open this door."

And I hit the send button. The next day in the hotel, I opened her email reply. And by the grace of God, she approved my request. On July 28, I was allowed to move in with my mom. My lawyer told me I was *very lucky*, but I knew better. It wasn't luck. It was God.

I moved in with my parents, back to my old room, which was now a guest room. While it felt good to be home in a familiar place, it was strangely awkward to be there. I had been married for over ten years at that point. It was weird to live with my parents and not able to bring my husband or my kids over. Not to mention we were all a little scared to talk about what had happened, I think.

Social services approved my visits with Lucas to be at my parent's house since he was still a "nursing baby." However, my attempts at bonding were futile since he was being formula-fed at home. My cousin would drop him off for me to visit every other day while my aunt stayed home with David. I began alternating the visits every other day to spend more time with each of them.

The first few times at my mom's house, I noticed a white van with black-tinted windows parked outside, seemingly always there when I would "transfer" Lucas back to my cousin. Every week, I had to send a visitation log/schedule to my caseworker, stating exactly when and where I would be visiting the boys. Art told me from the get-go not to spend one minute over that time, or they would use it against me.

Here we were at nearly the one-month mark since this nightmare began, and nothing had changed. I called Art regularly for updates on the criminal investigation. They kept telling us it was an open investigation, so information could not be disclosed. He subpoenaed the police report six times, and his requests were always denied.

14

Pretrial Meetings and Lie Detectors

O n August 3, we had a one-month review hearing to let the judge know what progress had been made, introduce any new evidence, etc. I brought all my "report cards"—my progress reports from the individual counseling sessions and the parenting and child abuse classes.

I felt confident that all the social workers had nothing but positive things to say about my husband and me, as did my counselor and the group facilitators. I received positive reviews from the psychiatric evaluation, and my sons were thriving under their father's care. *This must be the day the judge closes this case*, I thought.

Art showed up, asked me for all the paperwork, and we went in. We all received a supplemental report with the updated social worker's narratives, the CRISP recommendations, and updates on medical statuses. But alas, there were still no police reports or updates on the criminal investigations. I went outside in the hallway to read this report. Although no official police reports were in the document, there were snippets of it in the social worker's communications with law enforcement.

This was the first time I had seen any mention of the nanny. The report read: "The [Doula] stated when she left the baby's home in the morning, the baby was fine."

I thought, *That doesn't even make sense! Why would I have told her to go home early and woken up at 4 a.m. if the "baby was fine?"* I kept reading and found that the same detective who had interviewed me the night of July 8 spoke to the nanny on July 16 … after they had already seized my children. *In other words, no investigation had taken place prior to removing my children.* They waited nearly one week to interview the nanny, who they knew was a possible perpetrator.

Once again, I'd been misled and lied to regarding this "open investigation" that they refused to give us the reports about. As I continued reading, something popped out. It was noted that the nanny's daughter (name redacted) had a "slight bruise under her eye." Per the report, the nanny reported that she had just finished working and was sleeping when the child fell from her bed.

As I read this, I thought, *So wait a minute here. You're telling me that my son David, who had no bruises, no signs of abuse whatsoever, was removed from his grandmother's care at 2 a.m. and taken to the county shelter—and yet this woman's child had a visible bruise on her face, and you did nothing? Wasn't this a child abuse investigation, and wasn't she one of the possible perpetrators?*

My blood began to boil, but I kept reading. The detectives also requested that the nanny take a polygraph, to which she complied, but her results were inconclusive. Detective Cruz stated in the report that "She [the doula] would not be able to be cleared without a better result." The detective went on to say that she had tried to have the nanny retake the polygraph, but she declined, which then brought the investigation to a standstill.

I was stunned, mad, and speechless at all these "new" revelations, and yet my family was still being punished, I was still being assumed guilty. *Why isn't anyone doing anything? If this investigation is at a "standstill," why am I still presumed guilty?*

By the end of this hearing, nothing had changed. We had a pretrial and trial date scheduled for August 13 and 24, respectively. Art immediately pulled me aside as we were walking out and whispered while covering his mouth, "Will you take a polygraph?"

"Of course!"

"Okay, I don't want you talking about this to anyone! You hear me? *No one!*"

79

By now, I had learned to just nod when he was ranting at me. "Call Doctor So-and-So to set up an appointment. You're paying for this with your own money, you understand? Tell him to send the results directly to me. You don't tell anyone."

Again, I just nodded. I drove back to my mom's house and immediately started googling the polygrapher. It turned out his office was in Beverly Hills, and he'd been an expert witness in some pretty high-profile cases. While reading about cases, that all too familiar thought was scrolling through my brain, *This can't be real. I've been through psychiatric evaluations, parenting classes, child abuse classes, and counseling. And now I have to take a lie detector test? Really? God, when is this going to end? How am I ever going to prove I didn't do this?*

On August 18 at 12:00 noon, I had an appointment to take the test. Fred offered to drive me down to the polygrapher's office. I had never been so nervous in my life. I knew I was innocent, but what if my body did something weird? Those squiggly little needles would measure my every breath, heartbeat, and move.

Fred tried to console me, "You'll be just fine."

And I thought, *This isn't the first time my physical body has failed me*—remembering my seizures, miscarriages, and other occurrences when my body seemed to have a mind of its own.

We arrived at the location, and Fred walked me to the room. "Remember, keep the faith," he said and went back to his parked car. The polygrapher and I introduced ourselves, and he asked me to take a seat on a sofa next to the wall.

"How are you feeling today?" he asked. "It's perfectly normal to be nervous. Anyone in this situation would be."

I just nodded. Prior to our meeting, he had asked me to send him a summary of my case and why I needed his services.

"I read your email, and from what I understand, the court is accusing you of having abused your child, is that correct?"

Again, I just nodded.

He went on to explain the science behind the polygraph and the common myths associated with it.

"What is really being measured is the physiological changes that are occurring in your body. Even sweat glands are detected through your fingers. And we're measuring your brain activity because when you're lying, you're basically making up a story in your head, and your brain has no memory of that actual story. When your brain is trying to find where that story is stored, your heartbeat actually speeds up because your brain is looking for it. Yet when you're telling the truth, you have the memory. Your brain has that memory, and it goes directly to where it is, and you answer the question, and your heart rate remains the same. Like I said, anyone in this scenario would be nervous. What the machine is measuring are physiological changes manifest in your breathing patterns, heartbeat, and sweat glands. When your brain is searching for something that didn't happen (a lie), your body physiologically changes."

He went on to explain the questions he would ask me. There were three types of questions: The control question, the relevant question, and the relevant control question. He was going to ask me three of each kind for a total of nine questions. The first question (Control) was something very simple and obvious to establish a baseline. He'd ask me, "Are you sitting down? Are we currently in Los Angeles? Is today Tuesday?"

Then for the relevant question specifically related to my case. "Did you cause those head injuries to your son Lucas? Did you cause those head injuries to your son Lucas on July 8, 2015? Did you do anything at all to cause Lucas's head injuries?"

And finally, the control question, in which you are supposed to lie. In these scenarios, he told me to listen to the question, pause, and visualize what I was answering, signaling to my brain this was a "made up" scene where I was lying.

It was a lot of information to digest right before I was about to be tested. He asked me if I had any questions. I shook my head no.

He told me to sit down on a chair, with all the equipment placed neatly beside it and facing the camera. There was some type of pad on the seat cushion (to monitor body movement/activity), a pneumograph that wrapped around my entire chest (used to measure respiration rate, and heartbeat), a blood pressure cuff, and skin conductivity sensors attached to my fingers (measures perspiration). This machine did not have the squiggly needles; everything was digital.

He had me "strapped in." I felt like I was in a straitjacket. My heart was beating as if it was going to jump out of my mouth, and I was trembling inside.

He asked me if I was ready.

"As ready as I'll ever be," I replied.

He turned on the camera. His voice changed as he spoke directly into it, saying his name, the date and time, and my name. He held up the cashier's check I had handed to him, implying he was paid prior to the test results being given, therefore not influencing the results.

The test began, and all I kept thinking was, *Please God, don't let my body fail me now. Don't fail me now.*

Every once in a while, he would prompt me, "No deep breaths, please."

I felt like I was going to hyperventilate at times.

"Remember to think before you answer," he said.

And in my head, *Oh, my God ... oh my God ... are we done yet?*

About one hour later, the test was complete. "Okay, we are done. I have enough data points to give you a result if you can wait a few minutes."

I nodded. He took all the equipment off of me and told me to sit on the couch. "You needed a score of 6 or above to pass. You got a 19. I can say without a shadow of a doubt you were not being deceptive. You passed with flying colors."

I wanted to scream! *Oh my God, oh my God, oh my God! Thank you, Jesus! Thank you, Jesus! Thank you, Jesus!*

"Do you want this mailed somewhere?" he asked

"Yes, mail it to my attorney, please."

I remember walking down the hallway, my pulse still racing and a sensation of blood flushing through my face, neck, and torso. I walked into the elevator and back outside, where Fred was waiting for me in his car.

"How'd you do?" he asked with a smile.

"I passed," I giggled.

"Of course you did," he said as he hugged me.

Going home that day, I felt better than I had felt in a long time! Everything was lining up. There's no way this wouldn't get dismissed at our pretrial meeting on August 13th. I called Art on my way home from the polygraph. I asked if we were going to show the results to social services. He quickly shut that idea down.

"No! I told you, I don't want you talking to anyone about this! It's something we will keep up our sleeve for trial. But no mention of it before then, you hear me?"

"But I passed! Won't that make them have to drop the case?!"

"No, it won't. It will give them additional ammo to try and discredit the polygrapher. They will say you refused to do it with law enforcement, implying you had something to hide."

This was so frustrating. The fact that everything had to be done in secret, and any exculpatory evidence could never be brought forth to end this! I had to await the trial. While nothing changed, legally speaking, social services continued to make a series of demands. One of them was that instead of having individual visits with the boys, they wanted me to "prove" I could handle taking care of both children on my own. So, the visits became fourteen hours a week for me to see both David and Lucas at the same time.

At one of my "dual visits," my cousin told me she didn't know what was wrong with David, but his stomach hurt. It might have been from emotional stress. Lucas was having stomach issues at that point as well because he had been switched from exclusively breastfeeding to formula feeding, and he was not enjoying it. I made an appointment with a social worker who monitored these particular visits and reported this to the pretrial case worker.

It was hot in August, and I needed to be somewhere with air conditioning where I could contain these two boys. There would be story time and craft time at the library, so I decided to set our visit there. David, not even two years old, did not want anything to do with story time and would not sit still for two seconds. Instead, he ran around the library.

I pushed Lucas in the stroller, ran after the two-year-old, and told him to be quiet because we were in a library. It may not have been the best place for a meeting. The social worker walked about ten feet behind me, observing everything going on. During this visit, Lucas decided to have a poop explosion in his stroller. David also had an explosion in his diaper, and here I was, trying to not look frazzled. This was supposed to be the visit where proved I could take care of these two boys by myself.

I asked for the key to the bathroom and tried to find the wipes in the diaper bag.

My cousin was there to drive the boys back home while the social worker monitored the entire scenario. My cousin looked at me frazzled, not sure what to do, not wanting to interfere, knowing our every move was being documented.

The social worker, by the grace of God, looked at me and said, "If you need your cousin to help you, you can ask for help."

I said, "I can? Are you sure? I mean, I can do this by myself. I can do it."

She said, "No, it's okay. You can ask for help."

I jotted her words down on a piece of paper, making sure it wouldn't be used against me in the future: "She told me I can ask for help. Okay. I can do this by myself, but she told me I can ask for help."

I called Priscila into the bathroom, and we just started laughing, trying to clean the boys up. She hadn't brought extra clothes, but that was okay. It was a hot day, so Lucas stayed in his diaper, wrapped in a blanket. Then I cleaned David up the best I could.

And that was my one-hour visit in the library. When I put David back in the car, he was really crying, and the social worker saw it, but she didn't say anything. She went back to her car a distance away, still observing what was going on. Priscila drove home, and I wrote up my report. Every time I had a visit, I jotted down any notes and observations I had made, along with the details about the time, location, and social worker, to send them to Art. I sent him my notes and waited until we had the pretrial hearing.

That day arrived before I knew it. This meeting would be between Ricardo and me, our attorneys, our caseworker, and social services' legal counsel, but no judge. I was anxious and frustrated at the same time, thinking we would finally get to show them proof of everything—the psychiatric evaluation, the polygraph examination, the social worker's reports, etc.

Art had already popped my bubble when he told me none of this would be discussed or shown during this meeting, and I didn't dare open my mouth about any of it! Since the very beginning of this case, both our lawyers told Ricardo, "You cannot defend your wife. If you defend your wife, they're going to say you're putting her needs above your children's needs. So whatever they ask you, you cannot defend her." He, of course, had a hard time with that. My husband never, ever, ever questioned me, my innocence, or my character—never.

He was always by my side, but he had a different way of dealing with his emotions. Ricardo didn't have to go through the services or the criminal investigation, but he was with our two boys who were acting out and were not their usual selves. He was trying to provide for our family financially when our business was failing. We were paying our bills with credit cards. We were borrowing money from friends and family. He was just plain angry. I didn't recognize this man.

Art told us the point of this conference was for the other lawyers to "get to know you." It would be like a little Freudian therapy session among everybody there. Art told me, "I really want you to emphasize your faith and your upbringing in the church when you are telling your story or when you are answering their questions. I also do not want you looking at your husband when you're telling this. You don't want to make it look like you guys are corroborating or are feeding off of each other or anything like that. You are not to make eye contact with each other when we are in this pretrial meeting."

I said, "Okay."

The impressions made at this meeting would once again be read by the judge to determine whether we would proceed to trial or not. He told me to emphasize my Christian upbringing and my higher education. He also told me to steer away from my medical history. *Here we go again,* I thought. *Another interrogation.*

Ricardo's lawyer reminded him to only answer what he is asked, telling him, "You talk too much."

We went into a reserved room in the courthouse. Even though we had seen these lawyers before, I had never been up this close or shaken their hands. It felt very weird knowing these people had been doing their darndest to keep me away from my children, yet I had to act civil and put a smile on my face. Then again, maybe I shouldn't smile? I didn't know what they wanted from me anymore.

So, the "interrogation" began. (I put interrogation in quotes because, in legal terms, it was not an interrogation, to be clear.) Our caseworker, Jennifer, began the questioning, starting with me. She asked me my entire life story, basically. As I told her my story, in the back of my mind, I was thinking, *When we came to America, this country was where everybody in the world wanted to be. This country was known for justice. This country was known for right being right. Wrong being wrong. Yes being yes. No being no. This country was built on the Constitution, built on individual freedoms. Yet here I was in this place that was nothing, nothing, nothing, nothing like the America I grew up to know and to love.*

It was heartbreaking to realize that. I had put this country up on a pedestal, but God shook that foundation to the core and showed me that man's justice is fallen. This world is fallen, and we can try all we want, but His is the only Perfect Law. I remembered my epiphany song, "Knowing Jesus," and thought, *My only hope is in knowing Jesus. Please don't let me get weary in doing good because of God. Bless me even in this broken, fallen world.*

I talked about my background, my education, starting a business with my husband, and they listened as it went on and on. Then one of Jennifer's last questions was, "What do you think should happen to your case? What do you think should happen at trial?"

I thought about it and said, "I hope the courts recognize that I love my children. I love my husband. I have done everything and anything the court has asked of me to show that I will do anything for my children. I just want to be home with my family. I want to be my children's parent. I do not want to be their playmate. Visiting them for one hour a day is not parenting to me. I want to be there to tuck them in at night. I want to be there to give them their baths. I want to be there to read them their stories. I want to be there to make them their homemade food. I want to be there to hear my baby cooing and ahhing. I want to be a parent. I want this case to be thrown out, and I want to be able to go home with my family."

Then they went on to my husband, and honestly, I don't even remember what he said. I was in my own little prayer group. I'm sure I was surrounded by angels interceding on my behalf, on my husband's behalf, and on my family's behalf.

I felt like we had ended on a positive note. But there was one lingering issue still going on. Before this meeting, our caseworker had demanded that Lucas get another full-skeletal survey. Within two months, they wanted this infant, barely three months old, to go through another extensive exam full of radiation. As parents, we did not want to do this.

My husband and I asked Art after the meeting, "There is no reason to put our son through this. There are no signs of abuse. Why should we have to make our son endure this?"

The wise bully, Art, told me, "You have to. You have to do this. If you don't do this, they will write in the court report that you guys are not cooperating. What are you hiding? Why are you not going to give your son the full skeletal survey? They will not let you go home." Ricardo and I were praying about it. I spoke to our primary pediatrician, and he said, "I am a mandated reporter. I see absolutely no reason to put this child through this exam to expose him to more radiation than he already has had within the last month. I am not going to do it."

This statement came from our primary pediatrician, who, by the way, wrote me a character letter for the judge. He had followed us from the birth of David through the birth of Lucas. He met me in the hospital both times and was the primary pediatrician for both of our sons.

He said, "I can't in good faith do this." He was an ethical doctor who, as a professional, did not want to put our son through this.

I had to beg him, "Doctor, please. I know, I agree with you. I don't want to do this to my son. I would not hold you responsible for anything, but in the bigger picture, we really don't have a choice. They're making us do this, and if we don't do this, they're going to say that we're not cooperating."

He was still very reluctant.

I also spoke to another doctor who worked in the same office and had also seen us and seen our sons on different occasions. She said, "I agree with him. There is no reason to do this. I will write a letter to the court that we do not see a need to do this. As mandated reporters, as professionals, as pediatricians, we do not need to do this."

I said, "Okay, I will take that," and they wrote the letter.

I gave it to Art, and he said, "Nope, they are not going to accept this. They're going to require you to do this. But I will put this letter on the record, right in your files, so that we have proof that the doctors disagreed when we go to trial."

I gave a copy to my caseworker, and she said, "We will still require that a full skeletal survey be done."

I contacted the pediatricians again and told them that they just won't accept this. Against their own will and professional judgment, they allowed the survey as a personal favor to me. Time and time again, it was made clear these social workers had in their heads that I was the guilty party, and they would go to any lengths necessary to prove their point.

I saw in my CAT classes they had an obvious bias against biological parents, and there was really nothing we could do about it. Ricardo and I prayed that God would protect our son from the radiation, from any current or future side effects, as we subjected him to another medical exam. To the surprise of no one, everything came out clear. There were no other fractures, or other bruises, or anything in that little body, in that little baby. As painful as it was to put Lucas through it, Art now had further ammunition to use against social services.

15

Homecoming for Mom

After our pretrial meeting, nothing changed except to postpone the trial. Surprise, surprise. I was beginning to think this would never end. It had been over one month since I had been evicted from my house. Still on seven hours a week of monitored visitation with both my sons. Still taking all the court-ordered services. I had come to terms with the fact the nanny was never going to face justice, at least not in this court.

Our life was once again in limbo since my aunt Didi and cousin Priscila were about to fly back to Brazil. If they flew back, and I wasn't allowed to move back home, we were back to square one, trying to figure out who would care for our boys.

Our original trial date arrived, August 24. Since we hadn't received any written documentation of a new date, I called Art to confirm we were not supposed to go.

He told me, "Yeah, nothing has changed. The status of the investigation hasn't changed. The criminal case is still open. Don't waste your time. I won't waste mine."

I figured he'd been right about everything up until this point, so why would I question him now. I called Ricardo and told him what Art said, and he responded, "I don't care what he says. We're going." I remember rolling my eyes over the phone and thinking *I don't have the energy to argue anymore.*

"Fine," I said, "I'll see you tomorrow, then."

I woke up the next day, and Ricardo met me at my parent's house, where I was still living. The boys stayed home with Didi and Priscila. My mom and Marty decided to go with us, so we split cars, men in one and women in another. There were no words exchanged between my mom and me on that drive. I was not in the best of moods. Feeling like I was wasting my time, as Art had said.

My trusty iPod was playing in the background, and this time, a song in Portuguese got my attention—a song by Brazilian artist Kleber Lucas, called "Aos Pes da Cruz" which translates to "At the Foot of the Cross."

I began crying once more. Music is my soul's language. The song reiterates God's promises when we humble ourselves. We are to kneel at the cross, knowing that God is "merciful and gracious, slow to anger and abounding in steadfast love and faithfulness" (Psalm 86:15). *Here I am, Lord. At the foot of the cross. I am clamoring in your Son's name. Give me the strength, Father. Give me your mercy, your grace, your light.*

My mom, not so attuned to the song, looked at me, "What's wrong?"

I turned up the volume. We began an intercessory prayer in that car. Each in our own language, in our own groans. I hummed the song and repeated in my head *"For when I am weak, I am strong"* (2 Corinthians 12:10) as the tears streamed down my face.

We arrived at the courthouse, my mood now in a completely different sphere. Spirit-filled from the move of God in my car with my mom, I wiped my tears, fixed my makeup, and headed up the stairs to courtroom L23. As I walked down the hallway, I could feel the pain, the desperation, the frustration, the oppression that filled those quarters.

The Bible's words "for we fight not against the flesh" immediately came to my head. These families were surrounded by the rulers, the authorities, "the cosmic powers over this present darkness, against the spiritual forces of evil in the heavenly places" (Ephesians 6:12 ESV). This was spiritual warfare. I prayed for those families as I waited there, not expecting anything to happen regarding my case. About an hour and a half had gone by when my phone rang.

It was Art. "Where are you?" he asked.

"I'm at the courthouse," I answered.

"Okay, I'm on my way there. Might be able to do something today." Then he hung up on me. My look of shock caught Ricardo's attention. "What?"

"I don't know. Art said he's on his way and might be able to do something today." I hugged Ricardo, and we immediately started texting everyone we knew to start praying—the congregation in Brazil that had been fasting, missionaries in Africa, my family friends who lived in Switzerland, the First Assembly of God family I knew in Fremont, my current church family in Long Beach, and of course my friends who had never left my side throughout this ordeal.

I saw Art walking down the hallway towards me, and I got up to hug him. He pushed me away, "Don't hug me yet. I can't make you any promises," and without any hesitation, walked straight into the courtroom.

I sat back down, *Okaaay ... I guess I should know better by now.*

"What is happening?" Ricardo asked.

"I don't know. Just wait out here."

I don't remember how much time passed between that moment and when Art stepped outside with a pile of papers, marked and separated by yellow Post-It Notes.

"Sign this." He turned the page. "Initial this." Then back into the courtroom he went.

This back-and-forth went on for hours. I didn't even know what I was signing or initialing. I was just trusting God.

Art came out, this time with a huge stack of papers in hand. He plopped it down next to me, Ricardo sitting on the other side, listening carefully.

"Okay, here's the deal," Art began, "You have to be willing to sign this document today, the way it is written. There's nothing in here admitting guilt. There's nothing in here saying you did this. It's just the social worker's narratives, the timeline of events, the medical records, the timelines, your assessments, etc. I had them amend or remove altogether the notes that were false or inaccurate. That's what you initialed here," he said as he flipped through all the pages showing me my signature and initials. "If you're willing to sign this today, the way it is written, they will let you go home today."

I looked at Ricardo, and we didn't think twice! If they told me I had to chop off my leg that day, I would have done it.

"Yes!" I squealed.

"Okay. One more thing to sign here." He put the pile of papers down as my family and I embraced each other, sobbing all over the place.

I looked at him and smiled, "Can I hug you now?"

He opened his arms to me, and we embraced. "I have been doing this for twenty-three years. I have never seen them let anybody go home before trial. You definitely have a higher power working for you."

Yes, I do, Art. Yes, I do.

Finally! I was going home. My heart was overflowing with joy, gratitude, and renewed strength. I opened the door to my house and was received with open arms by my aunt, hugging me as tears gushed down our faces. I saw David looking at me in shock.

Priscila was talking to him in Portuguese, "Look, it's Mommy! Mommy is home to stay!"

He gave me a little smile, and my aunt stepped away and told him, "Go! Go hug your Mommy!"

I got on my knees, opened my arms, and he came running to me. Oh, how I had missed this sweet embrace. I wanted to freeze that moment in time. Lucas was sleeping like a little angel in his bassinet, the massive scar still exposed. I touched his tiny hand.

Thank you, Jesus. Everyone wanted to celebrate, so Ricardo put together a big barbecue party for everybody to welcome me home. I appreciated the gesture. I truly did. I knew everybody was so happy for me, but I was … I don't know—I was still processing, maybe even grieving—for the time I had lost with my children. This reminded me of when I was pregnant with David after having a miscarriage. Everyone was so happy I was pregnant again that they wanted to come to the ultrasound appointments with me, and while I knew their intention was good, deep inside, I was too scared to celebrate. Remembering the loss of my first child and getting attached to my not-yet-born David was challenging. The fear of another loss kept creeping in.

Although I was allowed to move back home, our case had not officially been closed. I felt like social services could still come in and take my children away at any moment. A social worker would be making regular visits to our home to monitor us. I remember holding Lucas and thinking, *I am never going to let go again. No timer. No monitor. His sweet little cheek on my chest. His warm little body next to mine.* My thoughts drowned out all the noise from everyone talking as I soaked in every millisecond of that moment.

At the end of the evening, it was time for everybody to go home, and I put my sons to bed. And of course, it wasn't the way I used to do it. My son David wanted Priscila to go put him to sleep, where she would sing to him, and Lucas would be rocked to sleep in my aunt's arms. I felt a little lost, a stranger in my own home. Even though the weight of the trial had been lifted off my shoulders, I felt like another trial in my personal life was about to start. I would have to pick up the broken pieces to put my family back together. Would we even be able to put it back together?

I remember waking up and, for the first time in a long while, being home, in my bed, in my bedroom. My cousin and aunt were going back to Brazil in two days. I lay in bed thinking about how amazing God's timing is. He knew everything that was going to happen and when. My whole life flashed before me—the loss of my father, the back-and-forth between the States and Brazil, my rebellious adolescence, my struggles in college, and meeting my future husband abroad … Everything that had happened, be it sorrow, heartache, rebellion, fear, unknowns, had all prepared me "for such a time as this" (Esther 4:14).

I had been under the shadow of my dad's legacy and my mom's faith. It had now been my turn to step out and prove my own faith. During this test, God never left me. I began connecting all the dots of all the other times He'd never left me, and I'd just never realized. I was not the same person I was before this started.

I looked at the calendar, where I had *everything* meticulously jotted down, to see my aunt's and cousin's flight information. I looked at the date I had been kicked out of my home, sleeping in the hospital, and the prayer meeting in Brazil that my aunt had told me about. It had been forty days in between.

Forty days and forty nights of testing. *Are you kidding me? Wow.* There was no clearer sign than that. If you have no idea what I'm referring to, pick up your Bible and read the fourth chapter in the Gospel of Matthew.

I got out of bed and walked into David's room. There he was, jumping up and down in his crib, with a smile on his face. My aunt hugged me. My cousin hugged me. My husband hugged me. Later that night, I took my aunt and cousin to a big evangelistic event hosted by Pastor Greg Laurie at The Harvest Crusade. *What better thing to do now, after all this, than to go worship God?* We spent the whole evening praying and praising God for the miracle that had happened.

It was then time to say goodbye. "Thank you" just didn't seem to cut it, after what my aunt and my cousin had done for me during that time. Tears mixed with hugs and kisses as we drove them to the airport, and they headed back to their home in Brazil.

God had shown Himself to me in ways I'd never experienced before, and through this new faith, I was going to be adapting to life after our ordeal. My children were going to be adapting. My husband and I were going to be adapting, and I was still going to learn more and more information as time went on. Not only learning about interpersonal relationships, trauma, and counseling but also learning about the illegalities of the child welfare system and the financial funding that it is linked to.

I could have closed this chapter of my life, and moved on but I had a fire lit inside me, which I couldn't squelch. Knowing all the injustices my newfound friends from CAT (Child Abuse Treatment) had experienced and that I had been one of the few to succeed in getting my children back, I couldn't stay quiet. I had to do something.

16

My House, but No Longer My Home

That terrible phase of our life was finally over—no more reoccurring court hearings or scheduling visitation appointments. No more monitored visits. My aunt and my cousin made it safely back to Brazil. I was home with my sons, and I could finally get my life back to normal. I had been back home since August of 2015, but our case remained open until February of 2016. We had been placed on what the court called a "Family Maintenance Program," where the social worker would come to our house in that six-month period and write up a court report at the end. During that same period, I was required to continue the CAT and PAT classes.

Life would never be "normal" again as we had once known it. Now, we just had to switch gears and get ready for the social worker who would visit our house once a week; she would later switch to once a month. This particular social worker, not one we had any contact with before, would write up the court report that would eventually go to the judge and make a final recommendation.

Lucas had been home with Ricardo, David, my aunt, and my cousin for close to two months before I was allowed to move back home with them. He was taking two anticonvulsant medications for his seizures. He had constant doctor appointments—specialists, neurologists, neurosurgeons, hematologists, and eventually physical therapy twice a week and speech therapy. For about two years, I constantly went to doctors, child abuse classes, parenting classes, and individual sessions. All while taking care of our daily family's needs.

During this time of constant doctor's appointments, I struggled with the mom's guilt of not giving my older son the attention I knew he needed from me. I knew he would remember more than Lucas would, but Lucas also needed my attention. Going to the appointments was considered a way to "prove" to the courts that I was actively involved in Lucas's recovery.

During those times, I had to drop David off at my mom's house, and she watched him while I spent the days going to the services or taking Lucas to doctor's appointments. When social workers would come to our house to visit, part of the agreement we signed was that we could not speak any other language but English with our sons during the visit. We were also not to use any type of physical discipline with our children. We were walking on eggshells, knowing that anything we said or did—if we even moved the wrong way—they could take our children again.

It was a very tense time in our lives. Art would tell me, "Every time the social worker comes over, write down what she said and what was asked; write down everything and keep sending it to me." The social workers were working very hard to imply that I had postpartum depression, which was the basis of their entire case.

This part of the investigation was related to the criminal case. However, it was not social services' business or legal jurisdiction. Art made that very clear to me. "I've pled the Fifth for you. They are not allowed to ask you questions about the case. And I don't want you talking to any law enforcement without me."

The social workers knew this, but they would sneak in questions, for example, "How are you feeling? How does it feel to be back home? Have you been to the doctor lately? Did you ever have symptoms of postpartum depression?"

They would ask me things in a seemingly casual manner, and I didn't associate it with being related to the criminal investigation. But when I would tell Art, he would bite my head off. "You do not talk to these people. Do not answer these questions."

I asked, "Okay, then how am I supposed to answer them?"

He said, "I don't know. I don't know." He would get very irritated with me.

Fred to the rescue. I would talk to Fred and say, "I don't know what I am supposed to say. If I don't answer, they're going to say I'm being evasive or I'm not cooperating. You know how they are."

Fred said, "Yeah, yeah, yeah. I know. I'll tell you a trick from the trade: When they ask you a question, you counter back by asking *them* a question. That throws them off their game. They don't know what to say after that."

Another childhood memory of some Bible stories came to my head. When Jesus was being interrogated or questioned by people, He always countered back with another question. *Huh! It worked for Jesus*, I thought.

One day the social worker asked if she could see Lucas's room. She looked, then we sat on the futon where the nanny once sat. She asked me again, "So how are you feeling? Are you feeling any stress being home, back with two kids? Must be stressful taking care of a baby who has just had a brain injury or brain surgery. How's your postpartum going?"

"Excuse me? What do you mean?" I asked her.

"Did you have postpartum depression?" she asked.

"What are you referring to? Like a diagnosis?"

She shuffled her papers around and replied, "No, I mean, have the doctors …"

"Are you asking me if I have a letter saying I don't have postpartum depression?"

The look on her face said it all. She was scrambling for what to say next and said, "No, no. Okay. So, you don't have postpartum?"

"No, I do not. I never did."

She quickly changed the subject, and from that point on, she never asked me anything regarding postpartum depression.

Being in that child abuse class and seeing all the different cases, I thought, *What if I did have postpartum depression? How was it in the best interest of the child or the mother or the family unit to rip a baby away from his mom? To deprive that mom of having access to her child without offering her any sort of support whatsoever?* It got me thinking, *Why does the system function the way it does? It doesn't make sense. If it's really about helping the child, if it's really about helping the family, then these people don't know what they're doing! Either they're incompetent, or there's another driving force behind it.* The old adage is true: When nothing makes sense, follow the money.

On a routine visit, Lucas's pediatrician noticed something that seemed quite harmless, to me at least. Lucas was always clutching his right hand, known as "fisting" in the medical field. He was referred to physical therapy, which began when he was about four months old.

Every time I went to the physical therapist, I had to bring in the social service forms to be filled out. The physical therapist filled out anything and everything about my behavior, my son's behavior, his progress, and whether I was listening to the physical therapist and doing the exercises at home. It was humiliating to have to take these forms with me everywhere I went, to have to email them to all these people who were *still* constantly watching me, knowing that any misstep I made would be used against me or somehow get twisted.

I had to do certain physical therapy exercises with Lucas at home. Simply getting him to open his fist and stretch out his arm was a struggle. I remember crying, thinking, *My son was born a perfect baby, now he can barely open his hand.* I had to put Lucas down at times just so I could cry. I couldn't bear to see my baby struggle. This made me more and more dependent on God.

One of the exercises entailed pulling his arms together, then out making a huge wingspan. I would say, "Super Lucas, Super Lucas." It would make him giggle. Day by day, month to month, we went from trying to open that hand, to passing the ball from one hand to the other hand, to sitting up on his own, to getting him to crawl, and eventually to walk.

David turned two a few months after I moved back home. We had a big birthday party for him at my mom's house. It seemed he was adapting well. I had already enrolled him in a preschool before Lucas was born, and the waitlists were very long. Now, with the demanding court orders and Lucas's medical follow-ups, and Ricardo working side gigs while we prayed about a "9 to 5 job," I had to put David in school. I felt so guilty, like I was abandoning him again. I tried to make up for it by spending extra time with him whenever someone could watch Lucas. Most of the time, that person was my mom. And when David saw my mom, he didn't want to leave her. He would throw massive fits, not a normal toddler fit, but one of massive trauma. He had fear in his eyes, and I can only assume it was a trigger of that night when he was taken from my mom's house to "that place." Sometimes my mom would have to spend twenty minutes in my car, calming him down before I could leave her house. It was so hard to witness. I felt inadequate and insignificant as his mom, unable to calm him. I was a trigger of distress. And I couldn't do anything about it, at least during the six months when a social worker was visiting our home, and we were being "watched."

17

New House, New Home

Our last home visit was sometime in February 2016. I remember texting all our trusted friends once again to start praying that this evening would go well. I remember asking God to calm David and please not have him act out during this visit, which would usually last around thirty minutes.

Toward the end of our visit, the social worker asked me, "So what have you learned through this?"

It felt like a trick question once again. I began swiping imaginary pages in my brain as if researching through a book, looking for the answer.

"I have learned to trust my instincts. That no problem is too big or too small to call a doctor immediately."

"What would you do differently?" she continued questioning.

"I would get a nanny cam. And not so easily trust people with my children."

She grimaced, as if she caught my not-so-subtle implication that I was innocent and would never have harmed my children. She began putting away her paperwork and said, "Well, as you know, this is your last home visit, per the court plan, and it's going to be my final recommendation that this case be closed."

We were happy, of course, while at the same time thinking, *What an enormous waste of time and money this cost us.*

On February 8, 2016, we had the final court date. Ricardo and I waited outside courtroom L23, anticipating that we would be going in there to finally see the judge! And maybe, just maybe, he would apologize (in my dreams, I know). Maybe say, "These are the wonderful things the social worker said about your family, and I am happy to dismiss this case …" something like that. I was expecting some grandiose finale.

We waited and waited and waited. Art didn't show up. Ricardo's attorney didn't show up. Then the children's lawyers, who were court-appointed public defenders on the case since the beginning, stepped out of courtroom L23 and announced, "Parents of Lucas and David Bruno?"

Ricardo and I raised our hands and stood up, almost as if we were two kids in grade school, eagerly replying, "Here."

She flipped through some papers and said, "Okay, sign here. And sign there. Your case is dismissed. Case closed."

My husband and I looked at each other and looked at her and said, "That's it?"

She said, "Yeah, that's it."

Still confused, we said, "Okay, thank you."

I walked out, thinking, *How anti-climactic is this? After all of this, all we get is a bunch of papers. Sign this, case over. Bye-bye.*

So, we went home. We had Lucas with us and I took a picture of the three of us in front of that justice center. The case was *finally* over.

Valentine's Day was right around the corner, and my mom offered to take care of our boys so we could go on a date. While on our date, we got an email from our landlord saying that she was going to sell the house and was giving us notice to move out.

Ricardo and I looked at each other, probably thinking the same thing, *"Really? Will these attacks ever stop? Will we ever be able to just relax and not have to worry anymore?"*

We had been in our house for about four years. We loved our neighbors, Mike and Kathy, who had been through this with us. David was already enrolled and going to a preschool nearby. But we had to start looking for another place, and as we looked nearby, we found that rent had gone up, and the houses weren't nearly as nice.

We were still technically unemployed. We ended up closing our business during this six-month period. It became unsustainable for my husband to travel or for me to do any customer acquisition/relations when all my time was now devoted to doctor visits, court services, hearings, etc. We were living off credit cards and any consulting gigs Ricardo could do on the side. Our home search led us to other cities, and the homes we found were significantly more than what we were accustomed to paying. We prayed, discussed, and concluded, "Well, if we're going to move, we might as well move up, right?" We ended up moving to a much bigger house in a nicer neighborhood closer to the beach. It was quite a jump up from our rent, but we knew, after all we had witnessed, that God would provide.

It had been our dream to have our own business and be financially stable so that we could have freedom and quality time with our kids, but having just gone through this crisis, Ricardo and I agreed it was best for him to find a full-time job, while I stayed home to take care of Lucas. We needed stability in our finances since we were in debt from all the lawyer's fees, the hospital bills, lost wages, credit cards, and we were rebuilding from ground zero.

David was still going to preschool close to where we lived prior. I didn't want to traumatize yet again by switching schools, so every morning, I drove about twenty miles back and forth. Lucas was going to physical therapy twice a week. I had to drive him over to the other side of town, but I always remembered my prayer at Lucas's bedside: "If I have to dedicate the rest of my life to taking care of my son, I will. And You will never hear me complain about having to take my sons to the hospitals, to the doctors, to the specialists, to the tests. I will do this. I will do it with joy."

I was determined to do it with joy, love, and gratitude that I was able to take care of my sons and that God had kept His promise when He told me that fateful day, *He's Mine. I gave him to you. Nobody is going to take him away from you.* Now I would do everything in my power to keep my promise, that I would dedicate the rest of my life to taking care of my son.

When this case started, we were going to buy a house. We had saved enough money for a down payment. It was a six-figure amount that all went out the window. Thank God that He knows all things. Thank God we *did* have that money on hand because that's the only way we were able to afford our attorneys pay for the polygraph test, the psychiatric evaluation, the CAT and PAT classes, and the individual counseling. Everything the court demanded came out of our pockets. If we hadn't had the financial means to pay for it, we would have ended up like many families I met in CAT and PAT. They simply didn't have the means to fight and ultimately lost their children.

18

Awakened Fire

Despite our Family Court case being closed, my criminal case remained open. Ricardo was very concerned about "these people," i.e., social workers, law enforcement, any mandated reporter, finding their way back into our lives however they could. He didn't like me contacting attorneys or talking about suing, which is what I wanted to do. I couldn't help this urge I had inside to do something. Anything. I had been enveloped in these cases, having attended CAT and PAT while home with my children. The stories I kept hearing over and over were nothing short of a nightmare. Even when my case was over, I kept in touch with some of my "classmates" to be a source of support for them as they endured the pain without end.

As husband and wife, I know we should strive as much as possible to make decisions together—to be on the same page when it concerns family matters, finances, etc. I had a very strong conviction about the word God gave me, that He would use my family, that everything I witnessed and lived would not be in vain. Our story would change families' lives. I had to speak. I just knew in my soul that I had to do *something*.

During the whole Family Court case, I asked Art if we were ever going to "get justice." He would glare at me and say something like, "Not now. Don't you dare mention that here. Now is not the time." As our case progressed, and as I saw what my fellow parents were going through, I came to understand what he meant. The Family Court system had no qualms about throwing parents under the bus simply because they could.

Now, I figured that the case was over, I could get some advice from Art. I had not spoken to him since our case closed in February; it was now close to June of that same year.

I called his cell phone. He answered, "Hey Rachel, thank you for the flowers you had sent to the office. That was very kind of you."

I giggled and said, "Thank you! It's the least I could do. Question for you: You had mentioned you knew a civil rights attorney who would sue CPS. Can I get his contact information?"

There was a moment of silence, then he howled, "Are you serious? Stop being greedy! Just be happy you have your children back!"

I was immediately taken aback. "Greed? You think this is about greed?! Yes, I have my children back, but that still doesn't mean I wasn't wronged!"

"I don't know what to tell you. You wanna open that can of worms, that's up to you. His name is Shawn McMillan. Tell him I sent you."

I hung up the phone and began bawling. Calling Art and ending up crying was par for the course now. Ricardo heard me crying and came downstairs, looking distressed, "What happened?"

"Nothing," I said, my voice cracking and the tears streaming.

"What?! Tell me."

I hesitated to tell him, knowing we were not on the same page regarding our next move. And Ricardo resented Art after witnessing all the times he had made me cry the past year. Art had just scolded me, and now I would get it from Ricardo.

"It was Art," I told him.

"Why are you calling him?!" Ricardo's tone was already changing.

"He told me I was being greedy!" I said as I covered my face, hiding my ugly cry.

"Greedy? What?" Ricardo said, completely perplexed, not understanding what I was talking about.

"You think this is about greed?! There's no amount of money in the world that can repay what they did to US!" I just kept ranting and crying. "This is about justice! This is about holding these people accountable! This is about every David and Lucas out there who don't have a voice! Rhianna, Diana, Ernest, Tracy, Jonathan!" (names of people I met in CAT). Now Ricardo began to connect the dots.

"Oh," he said while crouching on the couch next to me.

"I am not wrong, Ricardo! I know what God said to me! I know what I need to do!"

Still not convinced, Ricardo asked, "Isn't the criminal case still open?"

"I don't know, and I don't care!" I replied like a petulant teenager.

"At least make sure it's closed, and everything is clear before you do anything!" Ricardo bickered.

"Fine!" I said as my crying ceased, and I became just plain irritated.

Ricardo went back upstairs to his office, and I got on the phone. I was not going to wait and risk going beyond the statute of limitations, which was two years from when the case was initially opened—meaning July 2017 for us. Shawn McMillan was the best at his job, and I didn't want to settle for anyone else.

That day I started calling and continued to do so before checking on my criminal case or any other matter. I had to go outside our house where the trash cans were kept to call without Ricardo hearing me. Any discussion about suing the government would always lead to arguments between us. I felt I was on a mission, whereas Ricardo, I think, was still in survival mode, trying to protect our family at all costs. Our marriage had already been through so much at this point; I just wanted to avoid any undue stress. I called outside almost every other day for close to a month until finally I got to talk to Shawn McMillan. I explained what had happened and asked whether we even had a case.

He said, "Yes, I'll take a look at your case." He told me statistically what the odds were. He told me how long it was going to take, the costs of hiring him, then concluded, "If you're willing to move forward under these terms, I'm happy to take your case."

I was ecstatic when I got off that call! Thank You, Jesus, thank You, Jesus, thank YOU! I thought while jumping around the backyard by myself. Then it dawned on me I had to tell Ricardo.

19

A Conversation with David

How was I going to tell Ricardo? I knew his main concern was our legal "clearance" so to speak, regarding the criminal case. So I did the one thing I dreaded. I called Art. But this time, I called his office and spoke to his executive assistant, hoping she could look through the files and find the status of my criminal investigation. She said she would have Art call me back. "Okay," I said as I cringed inside. Keeping this a secret from Ricardo was torture.

Speaking of torture, dealing with David, now 2.5 years old, was a whole other form of torture that kept me awake at night. I knew he had experienced so much trauma, I couldn't even imagine. He had been ripped away in the middle of the night from his grandma, his mom, his dad, from anybody and everybody he knew, being taken into some strange place overnight, where only God knows what they did to him. He acted as if he was experiencing past traumas subconsciously—biting himself, pinching himself. I knew it was happening, but I didn't know what to do or how to deal with it. I felt the rejection. I felt the pain.

I felt the trauma as well. I had had my children ripped away from me and wasn't afforded the chance to defend myself. Every time we went to my mom's house, we had to relive the trauma.

Without realizing it, I started building a wall against my two-year-old son because he would say hurtful things to me, through no fault of his own, of course: "I don't want you, Mommy. I don't want you. I want to go stay at Dede's house. I want to go back to Dede's house. I don't want to be here. I don't want you. I don't want you." What I heard him say was, "I don't love you. You abandoned me. I don't trust you."

I tried to ignore the feelings of pain and rejection, pretending I didn't hear him. One day, while giving David a bath, once again, he began saying, "I don't want you. I don't want to be here. Go away, Mommy." This feeling of anger came from inside of me. I wanted to scream at him and say, "You know what? Do you want to go live with your grandma? Do you know how close that came to being a reality, and you would never see me again in your life!? Through no fault of my own. Do you know that?!"

Of course, I didn't say that out loud to him. I just stepped out and ran to the other bathroom, closing the door, and burst into tears. I cried and begged in prayer, "God, forgive me. Help me! Forgive me for giving the enemy the territory to sow bitterness and anger in my heart towards my son. He's the victim, but I'm a victim, too! I can't take this anymore!" Everything seemed so unfair. It was like the dam of emotions I had been holding for nearly one year had finally burst. I couldn't pretend or ignore it any longer.

As I sat on the bathroom floor, still in tears, I heard that subtle voice, You're the adult in this situation.

I covered my face with my hands, sobbed some more, and prayed, "You're right God, forgive me. How can I heal our relationship? How am I supposed to tell him? WHAT am I supposed to tell him? Help me."

I felt the Holy Spirit again. Talk to him.

People's voices lingered in my mind: He's too young. He doesn't remember. But the other voice kept saying, Yes, talk to him.

I took a deep breath, wiped my face clean, and went back to the bathroom, where David played in the tub. I got him out, dried him off, and put his clothes on to get him ready for a nap. I sat down on the floor with him next to his crib, which was a toddler bed now, and I asked him, "David, do you remember when your auntie Priscilla came over to take care of you?"

He looked at me and, the first thing out of his mouth was, "Why did you leave?"

That moment confirmed for me that he remembered, and he knew I had left—he knew something had happened. I went back to my room and grabbed my phone. I put him on my lap and began to show him the pictures on my phone of his baby brother in the hospital—Lucas's head all wrapped up, with tubes coming out, Ricardo and I at the bedside.

I told him, "Look, this is what happened to Lucas." He looked at the pictures. I'm not sure he understood what those pictures meant, but I went on, "They thought that Mommy had hurt Lucas, that Mommy had done this to his head."

He looked up at me, crumpled his eyebrows, and said, "You never hurt us, Mommy."

I said, "I know David, I know. But they thought that if Mommy had done this to Lucas, I was going to do it to you."

"Who hurt Lucas?" he asked.

"The nanny did," I answered.

"Is she in jail?" he asked in a very firm voice.

I tried to figure out in my head how I was going to explain this to my son without creating in him a spirit of rebellion or distrust or anger toward law enforcement, doctors, and hospitals.

"I don't know, David. But we have to forgive her. We have to forgive the nanny, the police officers, the doctors, everybody. That's what the Bible tells us to do. You know why?" He shook his head no. I went on, "Because Jesus forgave us. He died on the cross for all our sins. You and me, Daddy, the nanny, the police officers, we are all sinners and must ask for forgiveness."

He stared at me and then said, "Why did they do that? Why did they take us away? Bad people."

I said, "They're not bad people, David. They thought they were doing their job. They made a bad choice; it was a really bad choice. They thought that Mommy did this, and they decided to kick Mommy out of the house."

He was just listening, and I continued explaining, "But none of this was your fault, David. It wasn't your fault, it wasn't Lucas's fault, it wasn't Mommy's fault, it wasn't Daddy's fault, okay? Some people made really bad choices—they really messed up, and Mommy left because I loved you.

It was the only way I knew that you would be safe, that you would be with Daddy. In no way did I ever want to leave you. I never stopped loving you. I missed you so much, David. You and Lucas. I missed you so much. I'm sorry I couldn't protect you. I'm sorry this happened to you. Will you forgive Mommy?"

I was trying to hold back my tears as he nodded yes. I prayed with him at that moment.

I continued, "These people made a bad choice, but we're not going to let them get away with it, okay? We're going to fight them."

He looked at me, and he said, "You're going to hit them, Mommy?"

I laughed and said, "Yeah, we're going to hit them with a pile of papers. That's what we're going to do," remembering that I had not yet told his dad that this is what we were going to do.

From that moment on, it was a complete 180 for David and me. He let his guard down; I let my guard down. All he needed was closure; all he needed was the assurance that I didn't abandon him, and he needed the truth. It was amazing. The maturity of this two-and-a-half-year-old to really grasp and understand everything I was telling him. He really did understand. This was the start of a healing process for us.

II

Part Two

.

20

The Beginning of Justice

Sometime after this, I don't remember specifically when, I received a phone call from Art. I took a deep breath and answered the phone, "Hi, Art. What's up?"

He replied, "I'm calling to let you know the criminal case is closed."

"Awesome! What did you have to do?" I inquired.

"Nothing. They knew they had no grounds. I just told the DA (District Attorney) she did not want to go to court up against my client. I would humiliate her," he said casually.

I just laughed, picturing a very similar conversation he had with Detective Cruz while Lucas was in the hospital. He pled the Fifth for me and told me that under no circumstances was I to talk to the detectives or police officers without him being present. Yet detective Cruz kept calling me and leaving voicemails, saying, "I don't know why you're not returning my calls. I would think if you were really concerned about your son's well-being, you would like to cooperate with the investigation."

One day I called Art in a panic, "She's implying I'm not cooperating! She's going to tell the judge I don't care about my son! What am I supposed to say to her?"

He replied, "Hold on. You stay on the line, but I don't want you to say anything, okay?"

I said, "Okay," even though I had no idea what he was doing.

The next thing I hear is a ring tone. A woman answers, "Detective Cruz, who is this?"

"My name is Art LaCilento. I'm representing Rachel Bruno. I heard you wanted to talk?"

There was silence on the other end for a minute. Cruz, clearly taken aback, responded, "Oh, I didn't know you were representing her in the criminal case."

"Yes, I am. What do you want?" he said bluntly. And without waiting for a response, he said, "She's already given you a statement; what else do you want?"

"Well, I just had some questions for her. Why isn't she cooperating?" Cruz asked.

"She's more than happy to answer any questions while I'm present," Art quipped.

"I don't see why she needs you there. It's regarding the well-being of her son. If she was a concerned mother—"

"What are you implying?" Art asked, now raising his voice and changing his tone. "Are you making accusations against my client? Who are you to say she's not a concerned mother? Listen to me, if you contact her again without me being present, I will tell the judge you have coerced my client, you are biased, and I will take you down on that [witness] stand!" he puffed.

Silence. "Is Mrs. Bruno on the line?" Cruz quipped.

"Rachel, can you speak?" Art said.

"Yes," I bleated.

"No further questions," and Cruz hung up.

I remained on the line and broke the tension by blurting out, "What the heck was that?" as I laughed.

Art promised, "She'll never call you again." And she never did.

Now, one year later, it was the District Attorney's turn.

"Thanks, Art." I continued, "I got in touch with Shawn, by the way. He said we have a case."

"I wish you the best," Art assured me.

I hung up the phone; now I could finally tell Ricardo. Things must have gone down without a hitch because I don't even remember how the conversation went. All I remember is saying Art had the criminal case closed, and I had already spoken to Shawn and scheduled our initial consultation.

Ricardo was on board! I had terms of the contract in my head, but nothing on paper yet. It would cost us a pretty penny, a mid-five-figure sum, to retain Shawn, plus the ongoing costs of discovery. Money we didn't have. We took the leap of faith anyway, trusting that the outcome would pay off.

We took out a cash advance from a credit card, taking advantage of the "zero interest or fees for 12 months" deal. We had our initial phone call with Shawn, where Ricardo could ask all the questions to his heart's delight. We agreed to the terms of the contract, and the next day I went to the courthouse to get our case file and paperwork ready for our in-person meeting.

We drove down to San Diego, about two hours away from where we lived. Shawn was well known, having won many multi-million-dollar settlements. I pictured us headed to some high-rise building complex to meet a fancy, buttoned-up lawyer. But when we arrived at the destination, it was a residential neighborhood.

I looked at Ricardo and questioned, "Is this the right place?"

"According to the GPS, it is." Ricardo shrugged.

We knocked on the door, and a dog started barking. Shawn opened the door, and we shook hands.

"Come in," he said while trying to corral the dog. "Outside, Aida!" he said, pointing toward the back door and laughing. "I'm sorry, let's sit over here."

We saw several people working on their computers, with stacks of books and manila folders everywhere. We walked toward a large, rectangular table and sat down around it with Shawn and another attorney who was part of his team. I expected Shawn to be somewhat like Art since he was my first-ever encounter with a lawyer. I felt anxious and nervous, thinking, *I hope he doesn't go "off" on me.*

To my relief, Shawn was very laid back with a much better bedside manner than Art. It seems that being a father himself and having seen so many of these cases, he knew how traumatic it was to talk about. He went through the case with us, never hesitating to pause and answer our questions as they came. I teased him, laughing, "Art would have bitten my head off by now!"

Shawn laughed but very diplomatically admitted, "I couldn't deal with Family Court. Art is one of a kind." Everyone at the table could agree with that. Shawn continued, "Believe it or not, they (referring to the system as a whole) treated you guys with kid gloves. You're lucky you didn't leave that hospital in handcuffs."

I smirked at Ricardo and thought, *See? Art was right!* Something Ricardo had a tough time admitting throughout the case was that I could possibly go to jail.

"Art always told me I could be going to jail," I said, sighing.

"Yeah, he wasn't kidding," Shawn affirmed. "But back to this case, the main thing that secures this was the fact that neither social services nor the police bothered to obtain a warrant to seize David from your mother's house or to place the hospital hold on Lucas."

The hospital hold stated that we could not remove our son from the hospital without a court order. The same night David was seized, social services (Dora), and law enforcement (Officer Locker and Detectives Cruz and Sword) illegally placed a hospital hold on Lucas.

According to the Fourth Amendment to The United States Constitution, we are protected from unwarranted searches and seizures, which is what they did when they showed up at my mom's house in the middle of the night. In hindsight, we can only assume it was complete incompetence or arrogance on their side, but a blessing in disguise for us. If they had gotten a warrant or a court order, it would have made our case much harder to argue in legal terms. The other violation was of our privacy, as protected by the Fourteenth Amendment. Families have the right to live together with minimal government interference.

These two constitutional rights were the foundation of our civil suit. Shawn told us we would sue the hospital, the counties, and the sheriff's department. We would also sue the social workers, the doctors, and detectives as individuals. And whoever else we might find during discovery.

But one specific person was not on that defendant list.

"Why can't we sue the nanny?" I inquired.

"This is a civil suit," Shawn explained, "The only entity that can bring about a criminal suit is the government. What she did to your son was criminal, but they didn't proceed with the case. We're suing them now for damages (money). Does she have any money?"

"Probably not," I reckoned.

"Yeah, then you're just going to waste money deposing her. Even if the court ordered her to pay X amount of money, if she doesn't have it, she doesn't have it." He shrugged.

While it was disappointing to hear, I had to keep my eyes on the big picture and why I was embarking on this whole thing to begin with.

As we wrapped up the meeting, Shawn advised, "I would say you guys could win anywhere from $300,000 to $600,000 in a trial, but probably no more than that. I'm not saying your case doesn't have merit; it does. But you have to remember, we're suing what people perceive to be the 'good guys.' It's going to be hard to persuade them."

When Ricardo and I decided to move forward with this, we agreed it wasn't for the money. All we wanted was a clean slate. As I mentioned before, we were in the process of buying a house at the time all this happened. And now, we were over one hundred thousand dollars in debt.

I thought, *I just want to do this so that we can start over. If we could just start over clean, without this debt we incurred, then I'd be happy. That's all I want. And ... for these people to be held accountable."*

I glanced at Ricardo, and he answered, "Yes, let's do it."

We signed the contract. Shawn went to work on drafting the official complaint. We drove back home, feeling very optimistic and hopeful that good things would happen. During the long drive, I remembered a vivid conversation with Rhianna. I met her nearly one year prior at CAT. We became close friends at the time due to all the similarities and mutual pain we shared. During the long drive, I remembered a vivid conversation with Rhianna. She is the woman I talked about in Chapter 12. We became close friends due to our similarities and mutual pain. At that time, she had the same lawyer, same judge, same caseworker, and same hospital, but she never regained custody of her children. During one of our classes, I remember turning to her while she was crying about the whole situation, and I said, "Look at me. How many people can look you in the eye, and say, 'I know what you're going through' and really mean it? I can. I see you. I believe you. And I don't believe in coincidences. God made us cross paths for a reason. When all this is over, I will not forget you or your children. I promise you. Do you believe me?" She nodded as we hugged each other.

Now here I was one year later, recalling I was doing this for them—for all the Davids and Lucases and Rhiannas out there.

21

Discovery Begins

O ne day while at home, I received a large manila envelope with Shawn's return address on it. It was the official complaint! Opening the envelope and holding that "pile of papers" in my hand sent chills up my spine. I pulled it out, and on the front page, I read:

"RICARDO BRUNO, an individual; RACHEL BRUNO, an individual, Plaintiffs,

vs.

COUNTY OF LOS ANGELES, a public entity; COUNTY OF ORANGE, a public entity; CHILDREN'S HOSPITAL ORANGE COUNTY, a private corporation; DEPUTY LOCKER, an individual; DETECTIVE CROSS, an individual; DETECTIVE SWORD, an individual; DEPUTY LEE, an individual; DORA TODD, an individual; NIKOLA SPRINGMAN, an individual; SOCIAL WORKER DOE 1, an individual; NURSE DOE 1, an individual; DOCTOR DOES 1 through 2, as individuals; DOES 1 through 10, inclusive."

I thought, *Look at us versus all those people!* It felt like David vs. Goliath. These were no small players. I showed Ricardo, and we both let out a puff of air. Ricardo recalls us showing David the pile of papers as I reiterated the conversation I had had with him about us "fighting these people." We both decided to cement it even further and prayed over this pile with David, asking God's will be done.

David was now three years old, and seeing his excitement was so heartening. That may sound strange to some, but to me, it was a continuing affirmation that he understood what was happening. After our prayer, we signed the documents in front of him and headed to the post office, where we let him seal the envelope and place it in the mailbox.

Now the "fun" began–getting all the documents from the juvenile records and admission requests. Both sides send out questions to the defendants and to the plaintiffs. Ricardo and I had to answer questions—interrogatories—and provide documentation for all of it. Needless to say, it was a very long process. In the first files we got, many pages had been redacted("blacked out" or removed altogether).

I would call Shawn's office and ask, "How am I supposed to answer when everything is missing? I don't remember the specific days, times, people's names, and I don't want to make things up!"

Throughout the discovery process, I mostly talked to Shawn's associate, Adrian. He was a very nice young man, intelligent, competent, articulate, and patient. He was always very quick to respond and answer all my questions.

"Yeah, they do this. Technically they can say it's private information or third-party information that we don't need to know. But we do need to know. We're going to have to file motions for them to give us the unredacted files of your minor children," Adrian explained.

Once the motions were filed, we had to wait days, sometimes weeks to get them accepted and to obtain another file with the unredacted documents. It was a cat-and-mouse game with the defendants' lawyers. They would file motions against our motions, until finally the magistrate (judge) would have to rule, "No, plaintiffs have a right to know this."

We then got all the unredacted files, over 700 pages worth of documents, the police reports, the social workers' notes, their training profiles, my children's medical records, with still more to come. As I read through the files, and answered the interrogatories, I still had an inkling of hope that somewhere in these documents, we would find where the miscommunication happened.

I remember reading the Family Court reports and seeing things like, "Mother is not emotional enough, not exhibiting the normal signs of a grieving mother. Mother's just acting like this is a makeshift doctor's appointment," etc. They were hurtful then, but I was about to find out just how unscrupulous the key players in this case were.

One of the documents was Dora's report from when she illegally seized David from my mom's house. When it happened, we eventually found out where they had taken him. But we were just now going to find out, one year later, exactly what happened during the forty-eight hours in between. What I was reading seemed unconscionable to me.

Dora stated they had forced David through a full skeletal survey, an exam that takes an image of every bone in your body. Now, remember, David wasn't even two years old yet. He had just been ripped away from his grandma's house, had not seen his mom or his dad in twenty-four hours, and was surrounded by strangers. He was taken to the hospital—the same one where his younger brother was—and they tied him down to the examination table to take the x-rays because he wouldn't "cooperate" or "stay still." The purpose of this exam was to see if there were any broken bones in his body (the same exam they forced Lucas through twice).

Social Services thought they would prove we had abused him. It was heart-wrenching to read these statements. All I could picture was my baby being strapped down to a hospital table, like a bad sci-fi movie where "evil beings" were trying to force experiments on him. I kept reading and noticed checkboxes with options titled: warrant, court order, parental consent, other. Dora had checked off the box that said "other" and hand wrote "general order." At this time, I didn't know exactly what that meant, but I understood enough to know it meant they didn't have permission from anyone to do any of these exams. I would literally curl into a fetal position, pound my fist into my mattress, and cry, thinking, *How can these social workers do this? Who are the doctors? How can you perform something so incredibly invasive and traumatic to a child without their parents even there?*

Dora is the one who took David to Orangewood, the county shelter where he would spend the night, but it was another social worker whose name was not familiar to me—I'll just call him Judas—who took David from Orangewood to the hospital the next day. The department of Social Services (i.e. CPS in Orange County) has a contract with this hospital (the one we were also suing) to perform all "forensic medical examinations" in a child abuse investigation. Judas's narrative was that a younger sibling had sustained critical injuries, and it was suspected that this older sibling, David, had had his head thrown against the wall.

When I read that, I thought, *What? Who the heck came up with this theory? Now they're implying I threw David against the wall?!* It still leaves me baffled. I never said anything close to that to a doctor, a police officer, a detective, or a social worker! Where did he come up with this?

While part of me was enraged, the other part of me tried to rationalize. *Okay, wait. Is he talking about Lucas? Did he think Lucas was thrown against the wall? Maybe he just confused Lucas with David.* But if this was the case, why were they making the "older sibling" go through this when they knew the younger sibling was at the hospital? It didn't make sense.

I remember calling Adrian again, asking, "Who is this person? What the heck is he talking about? Can we add him to the lawsuit? And is he straight up lying or just incompetent?"

Adrian replied, "That's up to the jury to decide. We will look into him."

That little inkling of hope I had that there may have been some misunderstanding quickly started dissipating. Why would you make something up like this? Obviously, David was perfectly fine; there were no signs of abuse whatsoever. Even Dora said so.

I kept reading, and it kept getting worse. In that same visit, they gave David thirteen vaccinations without our consent, a court order, or a warrant. I'm not a doctor, but I can read, and I know that giving thirteen vaccinations at once is not something you do to a twenty-month-old child. Heck, not even to a full-grown adult. No sane pediatrician would do that. The person who administered the vaccines worked for the county at Orangewood. They're just "doing their job" and said David wasn't up to date, so they gave him all the shots to "catch him up."

We did have David vaccinated, but we modified the schedule after he had a reaction to one of the shots when he was an infant. We discussed it with our pediatrician and decided to space them out. There is a lot of information today about vaccine injuries. Whether you decide to vaccinate your child or not, I believe it is none of my business and is completely up to you as a parent. The least these people could have done was to reach out to his primary pediatrician and inquire why the child had not been vaccinated. The problem is no one has oversight over this government agency. As Art told me in the beginning, they don't follow Constitutional law and are told they can do whatever is in the "best interest of the child." Today, I have absolutely no doubt God had a hedge of protection over my son. What if David had had a severe reaction? He could have died from the toxicity of all these injections.

But they still weren't done "examining" David. I saw they had performed another exam called an "anal wink test." This exam is usually performed for sexual abuse. A probe is inserted into a child's anus, and they observe how it contracts. When I read this, I just wanted to run to school and hug David. Shower him with love and apologies. *What kind of psychological toll this must this take on a child?* I raged in my head, *If this isn't child abuse, I don't know what is.* They were digging for anything they could find to try to incriminate Ricardo or me. I would lie in bed face down on a pillow to muffle my cries. Feeling completely rattled, I kept repeating in my head, *I wasn't there to protect you. I should've been there to protect you. I'm so sorry, David. I'm sorry.* The guilt still haunts me, but I have learned to embrace grace.

After discovering these things, we had more to add to our initial complaint—under the umbrella of illegal search and seizure, we included Unwarranted Medical Examination and Unwarranted Vaccinations. During our discussion about the new claims, I asked Shawn, "Why would the doctors do this? Don't they know it's illegal?"

Shawn weighed in, "Well, doctors aren't expected to be investigators. If a social worker comes to the ER and says they suspect the child got thrown against the wall, then it's a doctor's duty to perform the examinations needed to make sure the patient is okay."

This was just one example of how CPS lies. These medical examinations were not revealed to us, the parents, when they occurred. They were revealed to us more than one year later because we were suing them, and we asked for the unredacted files. Had we not sued them, we may have never found out that this happened to our son. I remember mourning and accepting the fact that, *Wow, this really is evil. This is unbelievable.*

It took me back to the CAT classes and the people I met there. So many parents were frustrated, angry, and desperate. They would tell the group that their caseworker had lied about a certain event. Or that a social worker would call one of the parents' exes to suggest they report something that happened years earlier. So much deception. And yet, there was nothing a parent could do.

22

Discovering All the Players

We just kept uncovering disturbing evidence through the juvenile documents, cell phone records, the different social workers' files, email communications, etc. One of the most damning pieces of evidence we found was against law enforcement and social services. We legally obtained their text messages and cell phone communications. Ricardo and I worked on these separately, since he was now working full-time. I would spend all day on my bed reading these messages and then catch him up at night.

I couldn't believe my eyes when I saw the text messages. This was communication between Dora and her supervisor Nikola, prior to Dora interviewing me at the hospital on July 8, 2015. We know this because it was timestamped.

The thread begins with Dora texting Nikola, "Hey, I'm on my way to the hospital. Just got a report of an infant injury and infant has a sibling. The baby is in the hospital, has suffered a cranial fracture. Baby was with nanny, per mom."

She said "per mom" when she hadn't yet spoken to me. It turns out that the public health nurse, the first person I spoke to when I took Lucas to the ER, was the one who made the phone call to CPS. I am not blaming the nurse; it was indeed a serious injury, and she's a mandated reporter.

After that initial phone call to CPS, what happened next was out of the nurse's control. Dora was assigned as the emergency response worker. She spoke to Dr. Wong on the phone before arriving at the hospital. Remember, Dr. Wong is the CAP (child abuse pediatrician) who Art told me was the devil. Nikola (the supervisor) responded to Dora's text, "OMG. You think it was the nanny/doula?"

This seems to be everyone's initial reaction. It's the most logical one. But Dora texts back, "No. Think mom."

I shook my head, and read that again. *What?!* My eyes nearly rolled to the back of my head. *Wow. If this doesn't prove they had made up their minds before any investigating, I don't know what will,* I thought while continuing to read the thread.

Nikola responded back, "Oh! Ok ... [sad face emoji]"

Dora continued to slander my character replying, "Apparently never cared 20-month-old both grandmas did at night."

Another double take for me, *"I never cared for my 20-month-old son (David)"!?* I told Dr. Wong that I had seizures, which is why I had a nanny, and that my mom would help me on other nights when the nanny wasn't available.

I remember Dr. Wong asking me if I might have had a seizure while holding Lucas, but I didn't remember it. I told her no because I always had "auras." I knew when I was about to have a seizure. Then it got me thinking, *Wait a minute, Dr. Wong told me it wasn't possible Lucas obtained this injury by the nanny dropping him. But somehow, I could have a seizure, drop him, and injure him?* It was becoming abundantly clear to me that everyone working on this case had a common goal, and finding the truth was not it.

Then I saw Detective Cruz's messages and cell phone activity. On July 8, the day Lucas was hurt, Officer Locker asked me to wait for the detectives (Cruz and Sword), who were on their way to interview me. I waited in that room by myself until close to midnight. The text messages revealed that while they "were on their way," Detective Cruz, along with Officer Locker and Dora, were discussing the illegal seizure of my children. This occurred when Dora showed up at my mom's house, followed by Officer Locker, threatening my mom that she was "calling back up," remember? We now knew "back up" referred to Detective Cruz, whom Dora was on the phone with. Detective Cruz signed something called "the blues," also known as an "emergency warrantless removal," by claiming that there were exigent circumstances to remove both of my sons.

They were saying both boys were in a life-threatening situation and had to be removed, without ever considering that Ricardo wasn't even there when this happened, and they didn't even interview him. They also ignored the fact that my son David was with his grandma, sleeping, where no signs of abuse were found, which Dora admitted in the documents.

As if seizing David wasn't enough, they also placed the hospital hold on Lucas. I never threatened or insinuated that I would remove Lucas from the hospital. He was in a monitored facility 24/7, being cared for. What, exactly, was the exigent circumstance? There was none.

The amount of corruption, backstabbing, and deception in all of this just didn't make sense. Why would people be so motivated to remove children from their families?

I had to find answers, and through a little bit of research, I found something called the Adoptions and Safe Families Act (ASFA), signed into law by President Bill Clinton in 1997. The legislation provided federal funding to the states so children would not languish in foster care. This shifted the focus from reunification (still inferred in the law's language as their primary goal) toward promoting adoption.

Parental rights must be terminated before an adoption can occur, so ASFA sets short time limits for states to begin the termination process. When I read that, Art's words immediately lingered in my head—except this time it sounded narrated by a man reading a horror movie: "They will make it (the case) last longer than six months." Now I knew why.

Along those lines, "concurrent planning" is encouraged, where child welfare agencies (government or private) actively pursue adoption while simultaneously providing required reunification services. Exactly what they tried to accomplish with my mom—asking her to sign the paperwork for adoption before I had even had a hearing! My mouth would just drop the more research I did. It all made perfect sense now. So many organizations were involved in making money off of this system.

I also found out that the hospitals get money in the form of government grants for having a CAP (child abuse pediatrician) on staff when in reality, there's no such specialty in medical school. A physician can diagnose a cranial fracture, of course. But to put a time stamp on it and say what caused it would require a radiologist or a forensic pathologist, someone who specialized in such research.

We even went so far as to consult with an orthopedic surgeon to see if we could acquire an expert witness to testify later at trial. We were told diagnosing the cause of Lucas's injury would require a series of images, from the first ER visit to a year of follow-up images, looking at them over a period to pinpoint the damage. There would be many variables to consider.

But Family Court took Dr. Wong's word as written in stone after looking at one image in the emergency room. In our discovery, we found that this doctor had eight pending cases against her for falsifying medical records in court, yet she remained employed. This just illustrated to me it was never about protecting the children. It was all about money and justifying their haughty titles to maintain the cash cow of federal funding.

23

Discovering the Nanny

Discovery was such a long process. I had to go through *everything* piece by piece, page by page. There were over 700 pages in the juvenile records alone. Then we got the text messages and eventually got video of the nanny taking her polygraph. It put a lump in my throat. *Do I really want to watch this? I don't know if I can bear to see her face.* Shawn told me that I had to watch it in preparation for the depositions and, eventually, the trial.

As I watched, all I could think about was Officer Locker saying in his report that I was acting like this was just another doctor's appointment. I wasn't emotional enough. I wasn't grieving for my child. Then I observed the nanny's demeanor during this polygraph test. She was very chirpy and acted like this was a job interview. Remember, this was done about two weeks after the initial seizure of David and Lucas. It was all very "fresh." She didn't seem to be nervous at all. It was a completely different experience than mine.

As the test went on, it was really bizarre. There was a lot of giggling and smiling going on, almost as if the polygrapher was flirting with her! I could only see her face, not the polygrapher's, but you could hear it in his voice. I couldn't help but think that she was married to a police officer. Whether he had coached her somehow or whether the polygrapher knew him personally, I had no way of knowing.

I paid close attention, remembering how my polygrapher explained the science and background of the test to me. He told me usually, when a test comes back inconclusive, it's because the polygrapher doesn't know what they are doing or doesn't know how to formulate the questions correctly. The nanny's results were inconclusive, and now I could clearly see why.

In the middle of the test, she asked for a break, stating she was cold. I saw someone's arm reach over and hand her a blanket. She then wrapped it all around herself and covered her face, barely showing her eyes! I remembered my test, where I felt utterly exposed and vulnerable and had nothing to hide behind (literally or metaphorically!).

She interrupted the test many times. At one point, she asked for Gatorade, saying she hadn't eaten all day, that her blood sugar was low, and that was why she was trembling. So many little signs of how manipulative she was.

The test ended and she left the room, but the camera and audio were still on. I heard the polygrapher ask someone, "Is this what you want?"

The other person, a woman's voice, responded, "Yeah, yeah, yeah, that looks good," and closed the door. A few moments went by, and the camera was turned off.

I turned off my computer and sighed, hands covering my face but not crying. I simply felt weary, sorrowful, and betrayed. *Did I even have a chance?* I thought. While reading all the documents, a lot of doubt popped into my head. Every document I read was basically reopening a wound that wasn't quite healed yet. I had forgiven the nanny. I had forgiven law enforcement, the judge, the doctors, the social workers, and the system. But reading the documents and seeing that there really was no remorse on their part, and they felt justified in what they did, was so painful to me.

What if we lose? What if the jury finds that they were right in doing what they did to my family? What if we're spending all this money for nothing? And the ever-lingering question, What about the nanny?

But I had to keep moving, no matter how hard it was. Each heartbreak made me stronger. Every betrayal, every disappointment drew me closer to God. I was taken back to Sue's house, when I would lie in bed at night, tossing and turning and not being able to sleep. I would pick up my Bible and read the "little" books, like Jude and 1 John. I thought then, *These books are "tiny but mighty!"* So much wisdom and comfort in these short reads. They're what sustained me back then.

Now, feeling similar helplessness like I did back then, I turned to my "little books." I just swiped through the pages towards the back and landed on the book of 1 Peter. As I began reading, tears of joy started flowing down my face.

"In this you rejoice, though now for a little while, if necessary, you have been grieved by various trials, so that the tested genuineness of your faith—more precious than gold that perishes though it is tested by fire—may be found to result in praise and glory and honor at the revelation of Jesus Christ. Though you have not seen him, you love him. Though you do not now see him, you believe in him and rejoice with joy that is inexpressible and filled with glory, obtaining the outcome of your faith, the salvation of your souls" (1 Peter 1:6 – 9).

Thank you, Jesus. Always reaffirming me. I have been tested, refined, and I'm now becoming equipped. I have not seen You, but I know You. Rejoice. The joy is inexpressible. I giggled by myself. I sighed again, this time letting out the grief and breathing in new life.

24

First Settlement and First Mediation

After about six grueling months of discovery, it was time to begin another stage of discovery known as depositions. In layman's terms, a deposition is like a day in court without a judge or jury present. The deposed person must answer the questions under oath and under penalty of perjury. Like cross-examination at trial, the attorneys ask questions and the deponent answers. A court reporter keeps a written record and a video record, which could be shown to the jury (eventually) at trial. You only get to depose someone once, so it's usually a very long day since you want to make sure all your bases are covered.

Even though discovery was still ongoing, we had a court-ordered mediation scheduled in September of 2018, and trial was scheduled for June 9, 2019. We had deposed Dora's supervisor, Nikola Springman, Officer Ly (the peace officer who had been at my mom's house when David was seized), and Detective Sword (who interviewed me along with Detective Cruz, but wasn't in command of the investigation). These three depositions gave us some insight and information, but the big players hadn't been interviewed yet—Officer Locker, Detective Cruz, and the social worker, Dora, or possibly Dr. Wong. We did still find interesting tidbits here and there, like text messages proving that they (Nikola, Dora, Cruz, Locker) had gone back and forth amongst themselves before even interviewing me. They had already made up their minds, and they made a conscious decision to seize both our children without a warrant. They never bothered to talk to the nanny or my husband or reach out to anybody before making such a decision.

Documents show that Nikola Springman, the supervisor, performed manual overrides in their computer-generated risk scores. Had they not been changed, my husband and I would have been classified as "low risk," meaning we had no prior record, did not consume alcohol or recreational drugs, etc. But to justify the removal of our children, they manually overrode the system to list us as "extremely high risk."

While connecting the dots of the three deposed defendants, everything corroborated with our initial instincts that they really didn't do their due diligence when investigating. The medical overreach was brought up during these depositions. Questions about giving my son vaccinations and invasive medical procedures without our consent, a court order, without anything. It simply came down to the fact that they did it because they could. Not one person had a legitimate reason, legally speaking, as to why such interventions were necessary.

I need to back up to when we first started discovery. Remember Shawn telling me that doctors were not expected to be investigators? By the same token, the hospital had some liability, but not much. Before even starting the depositions, the hospital was the first to reach out and offer a settlement. I did not want to settle, of course, but at the same time, I always wondered why we were suing the hospital. I never felt judged by any of those doctors except for Dr. Wong. I remember the ER doctor's face when he came back to me, and he told me, "This is very serious." He was stern with me, but I never felt any sort of accusation. I could tell he was very upset at the circumstance under which he believed Lucas' injury had occurred. The neurosurgeon was always very empathetic towards me. All the physicians were horrified at what Family Court was putting us through.

But then we discovered that social worker Judas lied, perjured himself, and said he suspected that my older son, David, had been thrown against the wall.

The doctors performed all those invasive medical procedures assuming what the social worker was telling them was the truth. Even so, the social worker needed to present the doctor with some form of "permission" from either the judge or a parent. It turns out they presented a "general order," which basically gives the social worker carte blanche. It was a piece of paper filled out and signed by a judge, authorizing any medical procedure that the social worker requested. To make it more ridiculous, this order was dated 2008. Our case happened in 2015.

So to recap, a social worker lied to the doctor and presented him with a "general order" dated 2008. It gave the doctors permission to perform any medical procedure requested by social services. Social services then asked that our son undergo a full forensic medical examination.

In a way, I thought, *Thank God for this hospital. Bless all these doctors for everything they did for Lucas.* While at the same time, I thought, *What are you people thinking? Are you stupid? Can't you bother to look at the date? You can see that the child is perfectly fine; there were no signs of abuse. There were no bruises on David's body. And you get an order like this that's dated seven years prior, and you can't bother to look this up?*

The hospital offered us a settlement. They offered us something like $25,000 and I called Shawn, "Are you kidding me? Heck no. Why should we settle with the hospital?"

Shawn conceded, "Yes, I know. I get it. Yeah, this is a crappy offer. We're not going to accept this."

I was still on the fence and argued, "But I don't even think we should settle. Why shouldn't they be part of the lawsuit?"

"Listen. I know what they did is crappy. It's their policy. And this doctor, unfortunately, there's nothing we can do about this doctor. When it comes to trial, the judge is most likely going to throw out the hospital. The hospital doesn't have any liability. They were simply doing what they were told to do under the direction of social services, with that general order signed by a judge," Shawn explained.

"But it was dated 2008!" I bickered, then laughed.

"I know. I know," Shawn said. "But when presented with the scenario that the social worker presented the doctor—that your son had been hit against the wall and there might be internal bleeding and internal injuries—the doctor had to do what was in the best interest of the child at that point. A judge is not going to hold the hospital liable because they're not expected to be investigators. My advice to you is that we settle with the hospital, but we will make a deal with counsel. I know the lawyer. He's a very nice guy. I've worked with him before. So we will counter back at say $250,000."

I agreed, "Okay, fine. Can we make them fire Dr. Wong or something? Can we get something out of this thing besides money?"

Shawn said, "We can't have them fire Dr. Wong, but we can make them change their policies and make our settlement contingent on them changing them, and training for their staff."

"That's actually even better!" I chirped. As I've said from the beginning, this civil suit was not about the money. I wanted change. I wanted to spare future families from ever having to endure what we did.

We drafted a document saying that we would settle as long as the hospital no longer accepted general orders, that for a doctor to perform any kind of medical examination on any child, the order needs to be dated properly, and the order must specify what kind of exam and why. No more carte blanche for these social workers or law enforcement or even other doctors, whoever it might be. Shawn added another little caveat, stating, "We will settle with you if you agree to the policy changes, but counsel will have to attend all future depositions and refrain from asking questions during the depositions." This gave us a fly on the wall, so to speak, during the negotiations and wouldn't tip off the other counsel that we have already settled with the hospital. The hospital's counsel agreed to the all the stipulations in the offer, except for the cash amount. They countered back with $90,000. Knowing that this could be a long, drawn-out process and that the suit against the hospital would probably be thrown out anyway, we decided to settle for the $90,000 with the hospital. But they were always present at the depositions and at the first official mediation.

On mediation day, Shawn told us to dress professionally and be ready to do a lot of sitting and waiting. This was an all-day event. We showed up at 8:00 a.m. at the Ronald Reagan Federal Courthouse in Santa Ana. We had a third-party mediator, a law professor, who did this as a volunteer for "fun." He had no agenda and no tie to either party; he would be going back and forth between our room and the other party's room with offers and counteroffers. Shawn had worked with him in previous cases and seemed to have a positive impression of him.

Our initial ask as we started the day was somewhere around $1.9 to $2.4 million. Shawn said, "There's no way they're going to go for this, but we can always come down; we can never go up. This is our starting point, and we'll see how much back and forth we have to do."

The first counteroffer was $200,000, as I recall. Obviously, there was a big disparity, and Shawn laughed, saying, "Yeah, no, we won't come down. Tell them to give us a serious offer. We're not going to sit here and play games."

The mediator went back and spent a few minutes there. They were in there talking, waiting, and brainstorming. We speculated about what was going on in that room—oh, to be a fly on the wall of that room! The mediator came back and said they would come to $500,000. Shawn could see that this wasn't going anywhere very quickly. The defendants had Orange County's counsel (which represented social services and the county); they had LA County's counsel (which represented the sheriff's department and the detectives), and the hospital counsel all together in one room. They were trying to make what Shawn called a global offer, which was a lump sum where we didn't really know who was paying what.

For example, in the $500,000 settlement, 90 percent of it could have been coming from Orange County's fund. The other parties would pay the remaining ten percent, and altogether it total $500,000. Shawn explained that they do favors amongst themselves for doing this sort of deal. It's a way to stop the suing party from charging them as individuals or holding them accountable as individual entities. They each would have to get the money for the settlement from their own budgets.

So we sat there for many hours, and the most they would come up with was $500,000. Shawn came down to $1.8 million and told the mediator we would not accept a global offer.

Shawn wrote down the numbers on a piece of paper, saying we want $X from Orange County, $Y from LA County, and $Z from the hospital.

He explicitly told the mediator the individual parties were not allowed to discuss with each other the amounts they had been given. They would have twenty-four hours to come back with an answer. If they didn't answer us in twenty-four hours, or if they shared information, the deal was off the table, and they should prepare for trial.

This was it. Would they call our bluff? It was tempting when the $500,000 offer came in because, at our first meeting, Shawn told us we would be looking at a $300,000 to $600,000 settlement. It was exciting yet very risky since we didn't know what, if anything, we would be awarded by moving forward to a jury trial.

But now, we had much more information in our hands through discovery. The mediator came in for one final negotiation. I remember getting emotional and blubbering something like, "Sir, I respect your position. I know what you're trying to achieve. I get that. But this is not about the money for me. It's about me being able to look my sons in the eyes one day and telling them that we fought to the very end to hold these people accountable. We did not let them get away with it. Whatever money we make, we must be able to pay off everything we owe. I want to leave something to our sons, to show them what we did with this money. This offer is not going to cut it. I'm willing to risk making nothing but being able to tell my sons that we went to trial, and these people were held accountable."

He nodded, his eyes sparkled as though filled to the well, as he left the room to tell them what our best and final offer was. Ricardo and I left that meeting feeling somewhat defeated but trusting God. Our trial was scheduled for June 9, 2019. We still had another year of gathering information before then.

Within twenty-four hours, they denied all the terms of our offer. We found out through our fly on the wall that during the mediation meeting with LA County, Orange County, and the hospital, one of the counties had not even sent a person with check-writing authority to the mediation. They were playing games with us, seeing what we would accept, what we wouldn't accept. Even if we had accepted the $500,000 offer, they hadn't sent somebody with authority to actually write that check. It made us think, *Wow, these people are really, really ruthless.* It made us glad we hadn't accepted the offer, knowing that they were trying to play games with us, seeing how low or how far we would go. They were probably testing our patience and our financial, emotional, and psychological stamina.

Ricardo and I saw this as spiritual warfare. All these people were being used to test our faith, our closeness to God. Who were we listening to at this moment? Yes, of course, we were listening to Shawn. He was very experienced, and he knew what he was doing. But we were finally in sync with each other and listening to God every step of the way. It's really what guided our decisions throughout the process.

25

Dora's Deposition

Finally, it was time to depose Dora. All the depositions were being held at the Orange County counsel's offices. I remember waking up that morning feeling excitement and dread at the same time. Dora knew all along that what she had done to my son was wrong, and I was going to have to look at this person.

We met with Shawn in the parking lot before going to the office. He opened the trunk to his car and pulled out about six white bankers boxes, a bunch of *thick* three-ring binders, and his briefcase.

"Whoa! Is all that for today?" I chuckled.

"Yup," he said as he loaded everything onto a cart with wheels, and we headed up to the building.

I can write a whole other book just from the depositions, and it would take another ten chapters to get through. So I will just focus on the most memorable moments.

I remember going all the way to the top floor of this building, which was very fancy. The kind of building I thought Shawn would work at. There was a piece of paper taped to the door of a conference room, on it printed "Bruno vs COLA." Shawn walked straight to it, and we followed.

The room had a big table; at one end, there was a screen set up with the videographer sitting directly across the table and the court reporter with a computer sitting next to him at the head of the table. Shawn introduced us to the other people: two attorneys representing the hospital, one attorney representing Orange County and social services, and a woman sitting by herself at the other head of the table. It was Nikola Springman, Dora's supervisor. It was interesting that she came to witness this since she had already been deposed.

Then I looked and saw Dora in the "hot seat" right in front of the screen, directly across from the videographer. He was testing out her mic and lighting. I kept looking at her; she looked really different from what I remembered, but I couldn't quite put my finger on what was different. A very odd feeling.

The deposition began with the court reporter telling Dora to raise her right hand to take the oath. *Here we go*, I thought. Shawn asked a series of questions related to her experience as a social worker, her training, prior work experience, etc. Nothing was asked about our case specifically until after lunch.

I remember leaving the conference room for lunch and asking Shawn, "When are we going to ask about—"

He casually pulled me aside and whispered, "No talking about it in here. We don't want them hearing anything," referring to the other attorneys present.

We went outside, where various food trucks were parked, and found a secluded corner so we could talk. He explained there was a method to his madness. He first had to clearly establish that Dora had received adequate training in her position with social services on matters of the law when it came to violating individual rights. Things such as perjury, obtaining warrants, what exigent circumstances were, what the exceptions to the rules were, different protocols regarding medical examinations, etc. Now I could see where this was going. Once it was clearly established that Dora knew these things, why didn't she follow them when it came to the warrantless removal (seizure) of our sons?

Lunch break was over, and the videographer began by saying the time we returned and reminding the deposed that they are still under oath, and the questioning resumed. The moment I had been waiting for had finally come.

Shawn tells Dora, "Okay. I'm going to show you what we'll mark as Exhibit

No. 22—or 72 rather, to your deposition. It's dated July 8th, 2015, at 9:38 p.m. Is that right?"

Dora confirmed, "Yes."

Shawn continued, "It says, 'Waiting for detectives get to hospital. Can't make contact with nanny until clear with them.' First, did I read that correctly?"

Dora nodded and said, "Yes."

"Who is that writing? Is that something that is being written to you, or is that something that you are writing to someone?" Shawn continued.

I was on the edge of my seat, tapping my foot anxiously, just staring at the table thinking, *Come on!!! Get to it!!!*

"That was something that I was writing to someone," Dora admitted as she stared down at the paper. "I was texting to Nikola Springman, who was my supervisor at the time," she added.

There was a lot of back and forth about the timeline of communication between Officer Locker, Detective Cruz, Dr. Wong, and Dora. Shawn was trying to find out at what point did Dora "think mom," as we knew was stated in the text message.

Shawn then referred to Dora's investigation notes that had been provided to us during discovery, "But they [Dora's notes] didn't include your supposition, your speculation that mom, Mrs. Bruno, actually injured her child intentionally, did it? We don't see that in your investigation narrative or your delivered service logs, do we?"

"Objection," Dora's attorney piped up. "That's argumentative."

We could feel the tension in the room. I could see my chest pounding through my shirt, my eyes looking side to side as everyone awaited what was coming next.

Shawn continued, "What you thought before talking to anybody, other than Dr. Wong, was that mom did it, right?

"Objection. Lacks foundation, assumes facts not in evidence, misstates her testimony," Dora's attorney asserted, but did not tell her to not answer the question.

Dora said, "Can you repeat the question?"

The court reporter read out loud, "QUESTION: And what you thought before talking to anybody, other than Dr. Wong, was that mom did it, right?"

Dora responded, "No."

I'm thinking, How can you keep a straight face? How do you sleep at night? She had no expression on her face. She just stared down at the table.

Shawn then asked, "Take a look at your text message—actually, before you do that, when you say 'no,' you *didn't* think mom did it, did I get that right? *Your* testimony sitting here today at 8:33 p.m. on July 8th, you *did not* think that mom was the culprit. Am I understanding you right?"

Dora kept trying to evade the question, we could see her attorney was scrambling by asking that the question be reread. And every time it was reread, Dora went in circles without answering. And Shawn kept reiterating, "That does not answer my question." After about five attempts, she finally answered, kind of.

"I did believe that Mrs. Bruno could have been the person who caused the injury to LB [Lucas]," she blurted.

"*Could have been* or *was*? There is a difference," Shawn clarified.

Dora answered, "I didn't know who had actually caused the injury. I knew that it could have been Mrs. Bruno or the nanny."

"Then why didn't you tell your boss that when she asked you, 'OMG thinking it was the nanny/doula'?" Shawn challenged. "At that point in time at 8:33 p.m. on July 8th, 2015, you had already thought about it in your mind. 'No. Think mom.' Did I read that right?"

Dora answered, "Yes."

Shawn asked again, "'No. Think mom' means you, Dora Scott, thought mom did it. Am I understanding that right?"

Dora finally succumbed, "Yes, you're understanding that right."

Shawn concluded, "Let's take a break."

The videographer turned off the camera, and Dora and her attorney bolted out of that conference room. I don't remember anything else that was said after this. I just remember going home as the sun set, giving Shawn high fives on the way to his car. Ready for the next one.

26

Detective Cruz's Deposition

L ike I said before, I could write another book just about the depositions. I have twenty-eight hours' worth of videos. Maybe we'll have a movie someday. But for this book, I'm going to focus on the key players that led to the disastrous travesty for our family.

We deposed Nikola Springman with no great revelations, but her testimony corroborated evidence we already had. We also deposed one of the peace officers who followed Officer Locker to my mom's house the fateful night of July 9, 2015. When asked why he didn't say anything when he heard Dora threaten my mom with arrest, he simply replied he was "doing his job" to maintain the peace. At no time did he feel the need to inform my mom that she would not get arrested, knowing she had not committed any crime.

Now it was Detective Cruz's turn.

We went back to the same building, and I saw, Cruz again looking unrecognizable to me. At the hospital, when she interviewed me, she had her hair up in a bun and was wearing a khaki uniform. Now, her dark hair was down, quite long, below her shoulders. She had on a black pantsuit, looking very professional. I looked at her directly; she wouldn't look at me.

Shawn's line of questioning began much the same as it did with Dora—questions about Cruz's educational background, employment history, training, etc. Banal but necessary questions to establish a precedent for questions to come—particularly regarding her job as a detective. It seemed she was the one who persuaded the others to "sign the blues" (warrantless seizure).

Shawn began, "What do you recall about the restrictions imposed on you by the Fourth and Fourteenth amendments?"

Cruz responded, "My understanding is everybody has rights, equal rights. Obviously, I can't just go into somebody's home and just take any evidence. And let's see. Obviously there's a way to legally obtain evidence."

Shawn proceeded, "What's your understanding of exigent circumstances? What does that mean?

Cruz answered, "Somebody's life is at stake, or it could be safety. It could be somebody who is—in regards to, like, maybe somebody's—there could be, I guess, severe physical harm, not just—well, yeah."

Unlike Dora, Cruz didn't get visibly flustered when she didn't know the answer to the question. I remember Shawn remarking that she had been very well-prepped for this. Meanwhile, I was waiting for the questions regarding the investigation of the nanny. But a few more things had to be established before we got to that.

Shawn asked Cruz, "Okay. Focusing for a moment on exigent circumstances, in the context of the seizure of a child from the custody of its parents, do you know what the definition of exigent circumstances is in the Ninth Circuit? Have you been trained on that?"

Cruz answered with some hesitation, "During that training, the child abuse, I don't think they went into—into that. I do remember there was another time where they did offer warrant training, which was a separate class."

Her façade and lack of knowledge were beginning to show. I remember listening to this and thinking, *This is someone deciding matters of the law? Our civil liberties? Doesn't even know what a legal search and seizure is?* Mind you, she had been working for the Los Angeles Sheriff's Department for twenty-two years.

"Okay. And it's your recollection that in that general class regarding search warrants, you also would have covered the exigency requirements within the context of child abuse investigations?" Shawn inquired.

"No, I don't believe it was specifically pertaining to—to children," Cruz admitted.

Shawn continued, "So let's talk about that a little bit. You have heard of the concept that you can't lawfully remove a child from the custody of its parents unless, at the time that you seize the child, you're in possession of specific and articulable facts to show that the child is likely to suffer immediate and severe bodily injury or death and that there's no other less-intrusive alternative means of protecting the child from that specific injury. You've learned that, correct?"

Shawn kept asking questions and providing document after document, exhibit after exhibit, clearly demonstrating she had never received specific training regarding the seizure of children from their parents. It was a shocking visual of how ill-equipped law enforcement was to deal with these situations. Not only cases like ours, which occurred in a hospital, but what about domestic violence cases, where children are regularly used as pawns by the abusers? It was very disturbing to witness.

I must not have been the only one who was concerned because while Shawn was sorting through further exhibits, Cruz's attorney interjected, "We've been going a little over an hour. Could we take a quick restroom break?" Everyone agreed, but only Cruz and her attorney left the conference room. Oh, to be a fly on the wall where they went. This was the longest deposition of them all. The questioning started getting hotter when they returned.

"On your referral to the DA [District Attorney], you actually had two suspects that you referred for prosecution, right?" Shawn verified.

"Correct," Cruz confirmed.

"Who were those two suspects?" Shawn asked.

"Shannon King and Rachel Bruno," Cruz said.

Shawn hypothesized, "And the reason that you referred two was because you weren't sure which one was the appropriate one to be charged?

Cruz disclosed, "I didn't know which person—or if it could have been both—"

Shawn interrupted, "You didn't know?"

"I didn't know," Cruz admitted.

One more eye-popping moment for me. *You didn't know, but you still took my children?*

Shawn continued, "Okay. And the decision to do that unwarranted seizure of both children was made by you during that phone call with Officer Locker?"

Cruz said, "Yes. We made—I made that decision—to detain the minor and take him into protective custody. It was a discussion that we had."

This went on for a couple more hours, and the next thing I remember, finally, Shawn abruptly asked, "Well, who did you think did it? In fact, sitting here today, do you have a thought about who did it?"

My heart skipped a beat, as I had been waiting to hear this all day, but I wasn't prepared for what I was about to hear.

Cruz claimed, "There was a lot of things that were concerning about mom. And then—actually, there was probably more concerning things that I saw with mom than maybe with Shannon so—"

Shawn chimed in, "Let's start with Shannon now that you've outed her, too. What concerning things did you see with Shannon?"

"It was concerning when she didn't take—retake the polygraph," Cruz replied.

"What did you find to be concerning regarding Mrs. Bruno? Did you talk to Dr. Wong before you spoke with Rachel?" Shawn quizzed.

"Yes," Cruz conceded.

As I had suspected, all the information obtained about Lucas's injuries and what may have happened that day came from Dr. Wong. Detective Cruz reached all her conclusions before speaking to me.

Shawn continued, "So what concerned you about mom?"

Cruz accused, "She allowed the—I mean, the baby went out—went without feeding for a very long time. Well, the baby hadn't fed in—I guess, according to Dr. Wong or from what Rachel told her, the baby hadn't—I guess the last feeding was, like, at 4:00, 4:20. And the baby wouldn't eat after that."

"Okay," Shawn countered, "Is that abnormal for a baby who may be sick to not eat? Let me—let me back up. Do you have kids?"

Without thinking twice, Cruz answered, "No."

Cruz's attorney quickly disputed, "Objection. Lacks foundation."

Shawn said with glee, "It's okay. She answered the question. Of course she has no foundation. She has never raised a baby."

Cruz's attorney grumbled, "Move to strike."

Shawn replied, "That's denied. I got the information I need."

It was really hard to not burst out laughing like a little kid in the playground, *"Nah nah nah nah nah nah!"* while sitting at that table with a clearly uncomfortable attorney and Cruz. I wanted to cheer for Shawn but had to keep my composure.

"Don't ask any more personal questions," Cruz's attorney griped. "That's inappropriate."

Shawn quipped, "Hey, our personal experiences drive our decision-making. I think it's wide open."

Even if it was taken off the record, it was so rewarding for Ricardo, Shawn, and me to confirm what we suspected all along: These individuals had no clue what it was like to raise a child. Shawn went on to ask a series of questions relating to baby care in general, illustrating that a baby who cries or doesn't eat has nothing to do with the seriousness of an injury or illness.

Shawn said, "Well, I have two children of my own. And guess what? Newborn babies get ear infections, they get snotty noses, runny noses, they are teething, they have gas, they have colic. It could have been a million and one reasons why a newborn baby was crying. Why was my client supposed to know her baby was crying due to a cranial injury?"

There was silence in the room. Shawn went on to say, "There is no reason, and you know it, why my client should have known."

Throughout this deposition, things just became clearer and clearer, from not investigating the nanny, to Cruz knowing the nanny's husband was in law enforcement, to admitting that it was concerning the nanny failed her polygraph—it just went on and on.

I got a glimpse of what she had said to Ricardo while I was sleeping at the hospital that fateful night.

Shawn asked, "Is it correct that that night when you spoke with Mr. Bruno, you actually told him that you didn't know what happened to his son, Lucas?"

"Correct. I remember that," Cruz replied.

"And did you also tell him that at that point in time, nobody was coming forward and telling you the truth about what happened?" Shawn inquired.

"I may have told him that," Cruz disclosed.

"Okay. So I'm correct, then, that whatever mom was telling you, you didn't believe her because you told Mr. Bruno that nobody was coming forward, telling you the truth? You didn't believe—I mean, you spoke to Mrs. Bruno that night, yes? And you didn't believe her?" Shawn echoed.

"Well, I didn't know at that time 'cause I still wasn't done with first speaking with Shannon," Cruz evaded.

"Well, if you didn't know, why did you tell Mr. Bruno that nobody was telling you the truth?" Shawn argued.

I don't remember exactly when, but during a break, I went to the bathroom and burst into tears. All the blatant lies and accusations about my character as a person, as a mom. It was so hurtful. I pulled Shawn and Ricardo aside and told them I didn't know if I could keep listening to this.

"Listening to what?" Shawn asked.

"Them talking about me and saying I should have known what was wrong with Lucas, accusing me of having done this to my son. Do they really think I would just let my baby cry for six hours knowing he was in this kind of pain?! What if the jury believes them?" I said while controlling my tears.

"Don't listen to them. When you do your deposition, you'll have a chance to tell your side. For now, just let it slide. You know who you are. You know what really happened. They're just trying to cover their butts at this point," Shawn assured me.

I hugged Ricardo and planted my face on his chest to muffle the sound of my anguish. He just held me.

Shawn tapped my shoulder, "We have to go back."

I wiped my face for what seemed to be the hundredth time that day and asked Shawn, "Should I go clean this up?" as streaks of mascara settled on my cheeks.

He said, "Nah-ah," while shaking his head, "Leave it. Let that remain on the video, for these attorneys to see, for the jury to see to be reminded of the pain, the pain that you went through two years ago, and it's still alive and well today. Leave it. It's a work of art."

I chuckled and thought, *Yeah, what a beauty I must be right now.* Looking and feeling like a hot mess, I mumbled the Bible words I knew, "Guard my heart, Lord," (Proverbs 4:23) and marched back into that interrogation room.

Shawn jumped right back in, "Okay. Am I correct that the only reason you removed David from the custody of both his parents, mom and dad, was due to the seriousness of the injuries to his brother, Lucas, and the lack of what you believed was a plausible explanation for those injuries?"

"Correct," Cruz replied.

"Now, Shannon King—you alluded to this earlier, but we didn't really follow up on it very carefully. Shannon King, her husband's in law enforcement, right? Did you do any interview of her husband to find out, you know, what she's like at home, how she treated her kids, anything like that?" Shawn inquired.

"No," Cruz answered unapologetically.

"So even though she was a suspect, you didn't follow up with her husband; you didn't go check on her kids; and you certainly didn't take her kids. I'm just trying to get to the bottom of why you took the Bruno kids, but you didn't take the King kids if you didn't know which one of these people was the perp," Shawn prodded.

"Well, I mean, because Lucas was the one that was injured, and I didn't know if it was mom, and she's the one that has—" Cruz began answering.

"So you just take her kids?" Shawn interrupts.

"It's just, I mean—again, I mean, it's the severity of the injuries. It's everything that I had mentioned to you. I don't know if it was her," Cruz admits.

One more time, the cohort in charge of this so-called investigation admitted she didn't know who did what to Lucas, but she acted as judge and jury, taking my boys away without further investigation. Despite how emotionally draining the day had been, we ended up feeling very good about what we were able to expose during Cruz's deposition. The puzzle pieces were all falling into place, as I still had my eyes set on June 9, 2019, our trial date.

27

My Turn

The day was fast approaching when it would be Ricardo's and my turn to sit in the "hot seat." But before our depositions, Ricardo and I met up with Shawn over a weekend to prepare. Based on his experience, he knew exactly what they were going to ask. He advised us on different tools or techniques for how to answer. He taught us to think through the process and not feel pressured to answer right away. Common sense things like body language and looking the person in the eye (not at the camera). We did these "mock trials" individually, without the other present, so we could each focus on our own story.

I went first. I met Shawn at his office, and he simulated a mock trial with me, playing devil's advocate. He recorded the simulation, then we watched it together and analyzed my mannerisms, expressions, and body language. If you ask any public speaker, even the most experienced one, they will likely tell you how cringe-worthy it is to hear or watch yourself on video. To this day, I still hate it. But it's what we had to do to make sure I nailed this deposition. No pressure.

We began the exercise of telling "the jury" in my own words what had happened that morning of July 8, 2015. Shawn instructed me, "I want you to close your eyes and picture that exact moment at 4:00 a.m. I don't want you to speak until you can see it."

So I did, literally closing my eyes and going back in time. It was very hard trying to go back into that space, into what turned out to be the worst day of my life. I was scared of what would come out. He then asked, "Can you see it?"

I said, "I can."

"Okay. So what happened when you heard him cry at four o'clock in the morning?"

I started telling the story without opening my eyes, yet I could see it. I was reliving it. Shawn told me he could tell when I was "in" by my body language as he watched and listened.

He added, "I could see when your arms relaxed. I can see when your hands open up and are not clenched anymore. We can see the change in your body. When they're questioning you, when they're asking you, I don't want you to answer them until you can see it. Until your body is brought back into that moment."

When we got to the part where I described taking Lucas to the hospital and being questioned by law enforcement (Cruz and Locker), my body started trembling, my voice cracking, tears streaming down my face. "I didn't know what was wrong with him. I didn't know!"

I opened my eyes and saw that Shawn was crying. Ada, Shawn's dog, was there, and she came over and started licking my hands. She always stood by and tried to comfort me when we were doing these mock scenarios. We did this for two days. It was overwhelming and emotionally exhausting.

Ricardo went the following two days, but we were not present during each other's preps. We would sit in the hotel room at night and ask each other what it was like. It was a whirlwind of emotions—from anguish to anxiety, defeat to denial, embarrassment to guilt. Pain. Panic. Rage. Regret. Sadness. Reliving it again through each other's eyes.

The day came for my deposition. Three lawyers were going to question me, representing those we were suing: LA County, Orange County, and the hospital (but we made a deal with them, remember?) Shawn had worked with them before. He knew their styles, what kinds of questions they would ask, and how to respond.

He particularly warned me about LA County's counsel. He told me she was not a very nice person, in not so many words. They had gone against each other in many cases; there seemed to be some personal "beef" between them. He told me to not take anything personally when she begins attacking me; it's merely the way she tries to break you down, but I shouldn't let her.

I remember praying that morning with Ricardo before we left our house and headed to the office building. The same people who were praying for us during Family Court were once again praying for us as we headed into a different lion's den this time.

The formalities began, and this time I was in front of the green screen. Shawn was sitting beside me to my left. The videographer tested my mic and the lighting as the court reporter set up her equipment to my right. The questioning began, and honestly, I can't remember most of the questions during that very long day. I felt like a broken record, being asked the same questions three years after the initial incident had happened.

But there were moments I do remember very vividly. There were some intense exchanges between LA County's counsel and Shawn.

LA Counsel began badgering me in the same way that officer Locker did, as to why I didn't intervene sooner with Lucas. "So you didn't call 911 then?"

"No," I responded as I heard her tone switch to a much more aggressive stance.

"You waited until grandma [referring to my mom] was going to come over?" she asked belligerently.

"Right. I didn't know what was wrong with him." My heart started racing, and I could feel my brain pounding to the beat of my heart. "I thought he was a gassy baby. I considered leaving David with my neighbor so that I could call the doctor. But my mom had told me she was on her way."

She callously replied, "And they said it was blunt force trauma? They told you it's either his head was hit against something, right, or something hit him in the head?"

Shawn interjected, "Objection. Misstates her prior testimony. Assumes facts. It's also argumentative and leading."

Feeling confused at this time, I replied, "She [Dr. Wong] didn't specify any—anything. She said it was blunt force trauma."

LA counsel continued, "Do you have an understanding of what blunt force trauma is?"

"At the time, I pictured a hammer to the head," I confessed.

Without a moment to spare, she asked cynically, "Is that what happened?" as if conveying that she had caught me admitting something.

"I don't know," I said, feeling unnerved.

"Sitting here today, you still don't know what happened?" she haughtily responded.

Feeling attacked and heartbroken, I responded in tears, "That's correct."

"And you have no speculation?" she relentlessly continued.

"No," I answered. While in my head, I kept thinking, Make her stop, God, make her stop! I felt an emotional breakdown could come at any minute if this line of questioning continued.

"So your understanding is that something hit the left side of Lucas' skull?" she asked again.

Shawn got visibly irritated and asserted, "We've been over this like four times. She's not going to change her testimony for you, but you can go ahead and try again."

I repeated my answer, "I didn't know what happened. I didn't know what my son was suffering from. I did not know." I can only assume I looked visibly shaken at this time.

She finally moved on to other questions but was no less contentious. She asked, "So that first interview in the hospital with Detective Cruz, she asked you if you would do a polygraph, right?"

"Right," I replied.

"And then, later on, you changed your mind and decided not to do it, right?" she quizzed.

"No. My lawyer told me—"

Before I could finish, Shawn quickly intervened, "Just stop right there. The fact of the matter is you [referring to me] did it later. She's not entitled to know who, why, where—well, maybe where, but not who and why—who told you and why you did it."

I looked at Shawn, and answered, "Okay."

LA counsel pressed on, "You refused to take the lie detector requested by law enforcement?"

Before I could answer, Shawn perked up again, "If they asked her attorney and that was communicated to her, then it's privileged. You're not going to get her to violate the privilege."

LA counsel rebutted, "I can ask the questions. I'm not asking her to violate privilege. I'm asking the questions in deposition."

At this point, Shawn had had enough and sarcastically quipped, "Yeah, I'm just wondering as to how this kind of aggressive approach is what you used on that last case you did up in LA." A case he knew she had recently lost. Burn.

"At some point, you took a private polygraph, correct? And you did not turn that over to LA County Sheriff's Department, correct?" she persisted.

"Correct," I replied.

"Did you pass? Were the results inconclusive?" she asked flippantly.

Finally, I thought, a question that can be answered and put her in her place! But then, Shawn jumped in, "Don't answer." I looked at him, puzzled.

"You're going to listen to your attorney?" LA counsel disdained.

"Yes," I said, not quite sure what was happening at this point.

"Assuming the results of the polygraph were that you passed, you would have turned it over to the juvenile court, right?" she asked reproachfully.

Shawn said again, "Don't answer."

I was confused and incredibly uncomfortable but remembered what Shawn had told me about this lawyer and how she would try to break me down.

"You're not going to answer?" she insisted.

"Don't answer the question," Shawn reiterated.

I felt like a child stuck between her two parents while they argued. Dad tells you to do one thing, mom turns around and tells you to do the exact opposite. In my mind I wanted to scream *I did pass the polygraph!!! Why can't I tell them Shawn?!?!*

"Well, if you had passed the polygraph, you would have turned that over to law enforcement to clear your name, would you not?" she accused.

Shawn was getting increasingly annoyed and protective, and he put an end to it all, declaring, "You're not going to badger her … she's not going to answer your questions. You're not going to badger her. If that's going to be your approach, we're done. You want to ask about a fact of the case, you want to ask about communications or interactions with your clients, fine. Let's do that. But you're not going to do this. Certainly not with that tone of voice, that attack. I don't know if that worked out with your previous case and his crew, but it's not going to work with me." He later explained to me that the polygraph was not relevant to this case. I'm not the one on trial here, trying to prove my innocence. If we were to release this information to them, they would have additional resources to go after the polygrapher and discredit him. He told me to let them think I failed. Then, when we went to trial, we could surprise them and the jury with the results.

LA counsel moved on, "You said that you don't know what happened to your son, right?

"Correct," I said, keeping my answers short and to the point.

"So it's either you or Ms. King, right?" she attacked me again.

I attempted to correct her and say, "They didn't ask me if I did it. They asked me what I think happened."

Shawn chimed in, "Hold on. We're not here to be involved in a high-strung argument. You need to tone down your voice quite a bit. You're actually sounding really … I would use a different word if it were a less formal situation, but you're sounding pretty aggressive. Almost angry, in fact. And I'm not going to let you put her through that. You're not allowed to yell at her and badger her. *I'm not going to let you put her through that.*"

She went on to quiz me with general questions, and just to add more spark to the fire, she rapid-fired, "You sued the hospital that saved your baby's life, right? And you sued the social workers, right? But you did not sue Ms. King? I don't have anything further."

Wow. I couldn't wait to take off that microphone, get up from that chair, and run out of that room. As soon as everything was finalized, I sprinted down the nearest hallway I could find, wringing my hands, trying to control my rapid shallow breathing, as a surge of emotions rushed through my body. I just kept walking as far away as I could get from that room until I reached a dead end and just crouched on the floor, crying.

I can't remember how long I stayed here, but I received a text message from Ricardo, panicking, "Where are you?!"

I calmed myself down and began heading back to the conference room. As soon as I saw Ricardo, I hugged him and began crying again. I felt broken. Violated. Attacked. It was like being in Family Court all over again, where the same players now with different faces were making assumptions about me.

28

Ricardo's Turn

"What did your wife tell you during that telephone conversation?" she asked Ricardo, referring to the first time I was able to communicate with him since he had been on an airplane the entire time.

Ricardo started.

"I remember she was crying on the phone, and she was saying, 'Ricardo, our son, our son, the hospital. He had surgery, and the doctors don't know what's going to happen to him.' And I said, 'Rachel, don't you worry about it. Let's pray. Lord, I pray that you save our son from the situation. Lord, have mercy on our son. We love him so much. Whatever is happening to our son, Lord, protect him and save him from the situation.' And I prayed in Jesus's name, amen. After that, I told my wife, 'Rachel, don't you worry. Our son gave us much joy since he was born, and he'll continue to give us much more joy. It's going to be okay. Everything is going to be fine.'

"Then she said, 'There's a police officer and a social worker; they want to talk to me.' I said, 'Rachel, talk to the police officer. Talk to everyone. Tell everybody. Do the best you can. Let's—I'm going to be there very soon, at 8:00, 8:30. It's okay. Don't worry. I'll be there very soon. Don't worry. It's okay. It will be fine.'"

Listening to Ricardo testify, things I didn't even remember he said, I couldn't help but thank God in that moment that I had a God-fearing man in my life. Someone I had prayed for as a little girl, who was my one "non-negotiable." My future husband had to love God more than he loved me. If my husband did that one thing, I knew everything else would fall into place.

That night at the hospital, Ricardo showed me to keep our eyes on Jesus, he calmed me down, he did what he knew we had to do. Pray. Had we not had our eyes on Jesus, I don't know how we would ever have survived such an intense attack on our family.

Orange County's counsel continued, "Do you need to take a break, or are you okay?"

"I'm okay," Ricardo calmly responded.

"When was the first time that you were informed that Lucas's injury was considered to be non-accidental?" she continued.

"I do not remember any doctor talking to me about that being non-accidental."

I must interject here to remind you of a reference from the Family Court case. Remember how Ricardo's attorney told him he talked too much? Well, this was a moment when Ricardo went off on a little tangent, but he had some valuable insight into what happened that night.

Ricardo was telling about events that happened while I was waiting in another room for the detectives at the hospital, so a lot of Ricardo's testimony I was hearing for the first time. It may sound strange that we had never shared our experiences with each other; we had, but not in so much detail. The events were just so devastating we used avoidance as our defense mechanism. If we didn't talk about it, it never happened, right?

He went on to say:

"What I do remember is—well, my first communication with Officer Locker, he—I was with him in a separate room right next to Lucas's room, and then he—he asked me, 'Hey, did you see the images? Did you get a chance to see it?' And then I said, 'Yes, I did.' Then Officer Locker asked, 'Do you have any other children?' And I said, 'Yeah, I have another son.' 'Well, you know, I think we need to see him.' And I said, 'What? He's sleeping right now. He's at grandma's house. You're not going to wake up my son. He's just fine.' Then he said, 'Oh, you know—you know, sometimes abuse runs in the family, you know. We'll have to check, you know.' And then I was thinking in the back of my mind, Abuse? What are you talking about? I was thinking in my mind. I didn't say that."

So in this instance, the officer had already given his opinion to Ricardo. Again, without ever investigating the nanny. This was within the first three hours of interviews at the hospital, between me, Ricardo, and law enforcement.

Ricardo continued talking:

"I just kind of didn't really understand what he was talking about. And at some point in that conversation, he said, 'You know what? This is so serious. It's like someone getting shot with a bullet, you know.' I am thinking, 'What? Shot with a bullet?' I don't really understand what he meant by that."

As I listened to this, I kept going back to that night. Seeing in hindsight how the entire time the officer, the detectives, were planting seeds of doubt, suspicion, and just plain tainted information in our heads.

Orange County's counsel interjected, "Did Deputy Locker tell you anything else during that communication?"

"To the best of my recollection, he asked me if I had any more questions, and I didn't really have any questions for him. I was just thinking what he was saying earlier was absurd in my head," Ricardo replied. Absurd is right.

After hours of questioning, we got to the part when I went to sleep after being questioned by Detectives Cruz and Sword. Ricardo is now recalling his experience, and I'm hearing it in this formal setting for the first time.

"About what time did you first speak with your mother-in-law after you arrived at the hospital?" Orange County's counsel inquired.

Ricardo began,

"I don't remember the exact time of my conversation. She called me and was saying, 'Ricardo, they want to take David, Ricardo. They're going to take David.' And I said to her, 'No. They can't do this. They can't take my son. They—we need to look for a lawyer or something. They can't. They can't take our son.' My mother-in-law is crying. She was crying. 'I don't know what to do. I'll try to find a lawyer. I don't know.' I saw Officer Locker outside of the room, and I said to him, 'Officer, there's someone trying to take my son.' He looked at me, 'Yeah. I tried to warn you earlier, you know.' 'You can't do that. You can't just take my kids.'"

I wasn't present at the time this happened. It was the first time I saw Ricardo's despair. I could feel my blood rising to my head, goosebumps on my arms. Ricardo pounded his fist on the table in anger and anguish. The glass doors in the room shook from the force. Ricardo's chin started vibrating. He clenched his eyes shut as the tears streamed down.

He continued, "You need a warrant for that! I need to find a lawyer! We're finding a lawyer! You can't!"

"Do we need to take a break?" Orange County's counsel suggested.

Ricardo was crying, I was crying, and we couldn't look at each other. The veil of composure we had been wearing was jolted off as this story reached one of its many climaxes. I don't think Ricardo heard the attorney speak.

He kept going and wailed about what my mother had told him:

"'They're going to take David, Ricardo. They're going to take David. I cannot do anything about it. They said if I don't let them take him, they're going to arrest me, and I cannot take care of him. I cannot do anything about it more.' We tried to find a lawyer. We couldn't find a lawyer. We don't know. I have to put him in the car. I have to help. He's not cooperating. He's crying."

Ricardo did not pause during this heartbreaking tirade, but I want it to be clear, he was reiterating the conversation he was having on the phone with my mom at the exact moment social services showed up at her house along with law enforcement.

Continuing his anguish,

"They cannot do this! They cannot do this! This is not right! This is not right. They can't take my son. He's just fine at grandma's house. They can't. They can't. They can't do this.' And then we stopped. We cried a little bit more on the phone. I didn't understand everything that was going on there. And that memory is what I can recollect."

Everyone was at a loss for words. What a catastrophic and devastating testimony for the defense. Can you imagine a jury witnessing a grown man crying, searing in pain after what these people had just done to his child?

LA county's counsel breaks the silence, "Attorneys, Shawn, everybody, do you need to take a break? Should we stop? Or should we go on?"

Ricardo glanced at Shawn, relaxing his shoulders, regaining his composure, and contended, "Let's go on."

Orange County's counsel continues, "Where was your wife during that time?"

Ricardo answered, "She was being interviewed by Detectives Cruz and Sword."

"After your wife came out of the interview, did you talk to her about your conversation with your mother-in-law?" Orange County's counsel questioned.

"No," Ricardo responded.

"Why not?" the attorney mused.

"Because that was a very disconcerting … I'm sorry. A very disturbing conversation. Very. I was not even believing what just had happened to us, and I wanted to make sure she would go to sleep and sleep the entire night and not worry about that. She could not do anything about it at that time. I wanted her to sleep, and I'd talk to her in the morning."

Shawn interjected, "You protected her."

The attorney glared at Shawn and continued, "When you had your interview with Detective Cruz and Detective Sword, did they tell you that Lucas's injuries were thought to be non-accidental?"

"During my interview with Detective Cruz, I started the interview very upset. I had just learned about my son David being taken away from grandma's house. I was really—and as I sat down and Rachel left the room, they asked me, 'Are you okay?'

"And then I said, 'No, I'm not—I'm not very okay right now. I'm not okay. Someone just took my son David from grandma's house. I'm not okay. When am I going to see him?' And then they would say that it's not their job. It's now DCFS's. Cruz said there was an investigation. Something was very serious. She said, 'And all we have right now is the medical, and from what we have, the baby was struck in the head.'"

Throughout Ricardo's deposition, there were a lot of repeated questions from all the testimonies done before (Detective Cruz, Dora, and Nikola). At some point, we did take a lunch break. During that break, I kept thinking, *What kind of "investigation" was this? It really seemed like they had already made up their minds before they even knew me. These depositions prove this. Why did they seize my son, force him through a full skeletal survey, and give him unnecessary medical intervention?*

Everything I was witnessing was so disturbing. I had flashbacks to that child abuse class. The parents shared over and over how the social workers made up so many lies about their cases. They made up statements. They spun their statements. They took things out of context.

We came back from lunch, and not long after, the defense "rested their case," so to speak, but Shawn had one final blow to give them.

He asked Ricardo, "At any point in time from July 9th until today, has anybody ever given you a copy of a court order permitting your child to be vaccinated without your permission?"

"No," Ricardo answered.

"How about those X-rays? Anybody give you a court order permitting David to undergo a full body X-ray?" Shawn probed.

"No," Ricardo said.

These were obvious questions Shawn knew the answers to, and we were sort of in the dark about where he was going. Then it came.

"Okay. What about an anal wink test? Do you know what that is?" Shawn went on.

"I don't really know, and it doesn't sound like something that he would need to go through," Ricardo responded, unsettled.

"Well, did anybody from the County, a social worker, maybe—anybody at all from the County ever come to you and ask you for permission to perform a genital urinary exam on either of your children?"

"No."

"Didn't one of these government workers suggest that David had been sexually abused, and that's why he needed a genital urinary exam, along with an anal wink test?" Shawn disclosed.

All three attorneys present simultaneously jolted in their seats.

"Objection. It's argumentative, lacks foundation, calls for speculation," Orange County's counsel decreed.

"Join and leading," Los Angeles County's counsel added.

"Join," the hospital's counsel contributed. Though technically, she wasn't supposed to, per the deal we had made at mediation.

"My answer was, 'No,'" Ricardo interjected.

"Well, if there's no allegation that you know of that the child was sexually abused, do you have any understanding why somebody would be doing these exams on your boy?" Shawn prodded. Once again, all three attorneys present objected.

Shawn continued, "It doesn't make any sense, does it? In fact, you weren't even aware that a genital urinary exam was done on your child not just once but twice at least?"

There was a series of rumblings and mumblings in the room.

Shawn rebutted, "Make a legal objection, and that's enough. It's on the record. It's preserved. And if you want to compel a protective order or whatever you want to do, we can take that up with the judge. But right now, here, make a legal objection, and then we'll get on with the questioning. So go ahead."

I guess the others then remembered they had no further questions. The questioning was over, the attorneys added their stipulations and terms to the documents. And it was done. Oh, what a relief it was to be done. At least our parts were done.

I remember going home that night and my body just aching, like I had run a marathon even though I was sitting all day. The tension in my neck, back, hands, and feet was palpable. It was a strange feeling, knowing I hadn't done any physical activity, yet my body had absorbed all the emotions I had lived through that day and manifested them physically. I took a bath later that night after putting the boys to bed. Everything seemed so surreal, like an out-of-body experience, reliving it again.

Ricardo and I prayed that night for the depositions of the other defendants that still needed to be done and for our trial scheduled for June 9, 2019—a full year from where we were at that point.

29

Defendant's Change of Heart

After our depositions, we continued the entire year of 2018 doing more depositions and discovery of the defendants. Now we were getting close to the 2019 trial date.

We had so much damning evidence after the depositions of key players such as Detective Cruz, social worker Dora, and her supervisor Nikola. But there was one key player left on my list, Officer Locker: the deputy who interviewed me at the hospital. His deposition date kept getting pushed out further and further due to scheduling conflicts.

Out of nowhere, Orange County counsel reached out to Shawn and asked if we would be willing to have another mediation. We had already had our court-ordered mediation. We could have simply said, "No, we are going to trial. We're not doing mediation anymore; you had your chance," which is what I would have loved to say.

But Shawn explained to us, "Okay, guys, they know they're in big trouble. After all the depositions and all the evidence we have, I think they're seeing the writing on the wall, and that's why they want to have a second mediation."

I said, "Great! Let's go to trial!"

He continued, "Well, I get what you're saying. And it's not that I don't think your case has merit. It's not that I think you will lose. You'll probably win. The question is how much. Juries are finicky. People are finicky. It's a toss-up. We never really know what a jury will decide and what baggage or biases people carry with them, based on their backgrounds or childhoods. They might not like the color of your hair, or the sound of your voice might remind them of their worst third-grade teacher. Whatever subconscious things we don't really know. And in my experience, having sued these people over and over and having gone to trial over and over, it's really hard to convince a jury. Because, remember who we're suing here—police officers, doctors, social workers. These are the "good guys." Society views them as such. It's hard to convince people that public servants went out of their way to be tricksters, to lie, to perjure themselves, to commit fraud."

"That being said, it can be done, and we do have the evidence to show; we just never know. Another thing, even if you do win at trial, the defendants will appeal, which means we go back to square one and start discovery and depositions again. You guys will spend a lot more money. You will have to call expert witnesses, not to mention the emotional toll it will to take on you and your family. We would be in this for another maybe two to three years after trial. My advice is that we go to the second mediation and close this out that day."

He must have noticed the hesitancy in our voices over the phone. It was so disheartening to hear. *Are they really going to get away with this AGAIN?* I thought. I've said it many times, and I'll say it again, this was never about the money.

I had the scene in my head all played out—we walk into that courthouse in slow motion with our lawyers holding their briefcases. They swing the doors wide open as the jury anxiously awaits the start of this trial. The judge, in his black robe, listens as we call witness after witness to the stand to be cross-examined, as "Eye of the Tiger" plays in the background. Maybe even a surprise witness at some point. The nanny. Her husband.

And we had not deposed Officer Locker yet. To me, the whole puzzle had not been put together.

Abruptly awakened from my daydream, Shawn said, "Listen, I get it. I would actually make more money if we went to trial! I love going to trial, and I'll be more than happy to represent you. But I can't do that to you and your family in good conscience. It would be best for you and your family to settle at the second mediation … *if* the price is right."

He mentioned other cases that went on for six, eight, or ten years and how going through this is emotionally and financially draining. Fine, I thought. It seemed to be the word of my life since 2015.

In reality, *fine* was *surrender's* rebellious sister. I had witnessed God's hand in everything from Lucas's recovery to me not getting arrested, to my children not getting adopted, to me going home. Seeing everything as God's grace is surrender, and no matter what happens, I continue to seek refuge in Him unconditionally.

We agreed to a second mediation with certain terms in place. Shawn called them back and said, "Okay, if you want to have a second mediation, we are willing to have a second mediation, but we're not paying for anything. We're not paying for the attorneys' fees or the cost of the mediator. Also, our offer will not be any lower than what it was last time. So if you agree to those terms, my client and I will agree to do a second mediation."

It was December 18, 2018, and there we were again, in the same place our nightmare was relived three months earlier during the depositions. This time, there were two separate war rooms. All the defendants' counsels were present—Los Angeles County, Orange County, and the hospital. The mediator came into our room, said something to the effect of, "Nice to see you again," and we started.

Shawn pulled out a yellow legal pad and wrote down two separate demands, one for LA County and another for Orange County. We demanded $1.4M from Orange County since we felt they were most at fault and $1M from LA County.

We had discussed earlier with Shawn, since we were most likely not going to trial, what else we could demand from them besides money so that other families wouldn't have to go through this like we did. He suggested we require changes to their policies and implement these standards in their training departments.

Shawn drafted some language changes to "warrant training" concerning the removal of children for the Sheriff's department since it was clear as day from the depositions that their employees were sorely lacking in this area. There were also changes for social services regarding the definition of "exigent circumstances" and "warrantless removal," as well as medical examinations. If I'm not mistaken, they had a period of six months from this day to put such language into place in their policy manuals and training proceedings.

Shawn wrote all this down by hand on the legal pad and handed it to the mediator. We sat in that room and once again speculated on what was going on in the room next door. Right away, Shawn assured us they would not agree to the amount we stipulated. Ricardo and I had a number we discussed beforehand; we would not accept anything less than $1.5M.

I don't remember how many times our mediator went back and forth, but it took a long time since the negotiating kept coming back with plus or minus $10K increments. Until he came one last time, saying, "They're getting pretty frustrated over there. Just as a fair warning, it's close to being their best and final."

I felt an unsettling little voice in my core, Don't be stupid, Rachel. Like the old cartoon with a little devil on one shoulder and an angel on the other, one voice in my mind said, "Don't back down! Make them pay!" while another said, "Remember why you're doing this." We made one last attempt to get them up to $2M, and this time I asked Shawn if he thought they would at least say they were sorry to us.

Shawn cackled, "Never. But I'll write it down here just to piss them off."

We all had a group laugh, and Shawn wrote our final offer with the demand of an apology from Orange County and Los Angeles County on their official letterheads. Even the mediator chuckled when he saw it. This was it. We either settled, or we were going to trial in six months. I kept praying in the Spirit as we waited, Your will be done, Lord. Your will be done. I felt anxious saying those words in my prayer, thinking, What if His will is not what I'm wanting? Then my heart would switch to, Even if, He is still good.

The mediator came back and said, "This is their best and final offer. They're not willing to come back any higher. They're going to walk away if you reject this."

The first thing we noticed on the piece of paper which Shawn had originally written on, before even noticing the money amount, were the scribbles on the lines where Shawn had requested an apology letter. They had completely blacked out the request. It was their not-so-subtle way of saying, "No."

The room resounded in laughter, "I told you they wouldn't do it!" Shawn grinned. I snapped a picture to have it memorialized for all eternity. It was like my four-year-old had gotten ahold of a pen for the first time and just went crazy trying to use up all the ink it had. It was a lighthearted moment in what had been an extremely tense day. Once the amusement wore off, we had a final decision to make. Shawn let us have our space at that time and turned his chair around to chat with his daughter (she was considering law school and asked us if she could watch).

The offer was $100K short of the bottom line Ricardo and I had discussed in the morning. You may be thinking, *What's one hundred thousand bucks?!* And I agree, on a logical level. But my soul was agonizing over this decision. I could feel my ribs tightening around my lungs and heart. I couldn't help but feel like I was selling out, as thoughts tormented me, *What they did was so, so wrong. Giving us money is such an easy way out. No one is going to jail. Nobody is getting fired. Not even a slap on the wrist. And we didn't even get to depose Officer Locker!*

Shawn reminded us that if we accepted this settlement, we could finally turn the page in our lives. This chapter would be over, and we could rebuild what they tried to take away from us. I asked him if I could talk about this if we settled; he assured me I could and *should.* That was another non-negotiable for me. I was not signing any NDAs (non-disclosure agreements, aka, "gag orders"), saying that I couldn't talk about what happened or disclose what was revealed during discovery. Ricardo and I just stared at each other for what seemed like forever, seemingly communicating through thin air. Then, we painfully succumbed, nodding at each other and saying to Shawn, "We'll take it."

To this day, I can't explain how I spoke those words. It's like my tongue was tied, and the words just came out by the Spirit. Internally, I was screaming, *No! No! No!* but my body would not respond accordingly. It all felt like a big haze. But once I said yes, Shawn immediately began closing and told the mediator. I remember leaving that building feeling like absolute poop (to not use another word). There was an ominous, dire feeling in the air. We walked to the parking lot with Shawn, and I kept saying, "I hate this. I hate myself. I'm so mad right now."

Shawn jokingly replied, "That's the sign of a good mediation. Everyone should leave a little pissed off. If someone leaves really happy, that means someone else really got screwed."

I guess that was some comfort, but I couldn't shake that feeling off for the entire weekend. I must have slept for three days straight. This was right during Christmas break, David was out of school, and my mom helped care for him and Lucas, knowing the difficult days we had just faced.

Ricardo convinced me to go out for dinner. We went to a new sushi restaurant by my mom's house when I received a phone call shortly after we had been seated. It was Rhianna, my friend from CAT, who had just had her parental rights terminated after everything she had gone through. I figured she was calling me for support, or maybe something had changed.

I answered the phone, "What's up?"

She responded with, "Nothing. I just wanted to tell you you're amazing."

It was like someone smacked my face. "What?" I whimpered.

"You're amazing," she repeated. I couldn't help feeling despondent yet embarrassed at my reaction to everything. Here I was, having just won one and a half million dollars, my children were home, and I was being comforted by someone who had lost everything. I got up from the table and stepped outside as I feel my chin quivering, holding back my tears.

"I feel like shit (*there, I said it*), Rhianna!" I shrieked.

"Why!?" she rebuked me.

"I should have gone to trial! These stupid idiots are going to get away with it again! I sold out to these idiots," I cried. My knees bent, and I eventually found myself sitting on the sidewalk with my back against a wall, my hair falling to the sides and covering my face like a cocoon.

"You're not a sellout. You did what you had to do for your family. And I still think you're amazing," she assured me.

"Thank you," I muttered. We cried together. I stood up and lifted my head.

"I'm not going to forget you, or your kids, I promise."

We said our goodbyes, and I walked back into the restaurant. Ricardo immediately asked what was wrong, assuming the same thing I did—that something was wrong with Rhianna. I told him what she had told me, and I just started crying again.

He simply replied, "You are amazing."

Then why do I feel like crap?! I thought, feeling such disdain with myself. I don't remember what else happened that night or during the days that followed. I knew it was just a matter of time before I had to accept the outcome of our case and our decision.

30

Epilogue

A nd That's What Happened. You've read it all. That's the story. How do I wrap this up in a pretty bow to say "the end"? I don't know. This incident, which lasted three years, taught me about so many aspects of life and made me reflect on what really matters. During those three years, Lucas's long-term medical status was still an unknown. Would he have brain damage? Would he have developmental delays? Would he have to be on antiepileptic drugs for the rest of his life?

I'm here to tell you we serve a God of miracles. Today, Lucas is six years old. Despite the traumatic brain injury, he is thriving in first grade.

Lucas only needed to be on the antiepileptics for one year once his EEG no longer showed any seizure activity. When he was two years old, he had to undergo cranial reconstruction surgery to permanently fix the fracture. In the follow-up consultations, his neurosurgeon showed us a CT image of his brain. Lucas has a lemon-sized "ball" that is encapsulated with fluid. That part of his brain is missing. I'll never forget the doctor telling us, "If I were only looking at this image. I'd be very concerned about this patient. But seeing him here today, in person—I'm happy to say I have no concerns whatsoever. He's a perfectly healthy boy."

This child has been through more than most adults will in their lifetimes. His name means "giver of light," and it truly matches his personality.

My other miracle, David, bore the brunt of this entire situation, in my opinion. Medically speaking, I am beyond grateful for God's hedge of protection over David. Those thirteen vaccines could have done so much damage, but they didn't. David is now eight years old, yet he has the maturity of someone much older. He has a keen ability to discern things of the Spirit. He's articulate, intelligent, and sweet as can be. His trauma could have caused him to be bitter, angry, resentful, and hurtful towards others. Yet, God restored all that was lost. David means "beloved." He is truly loved by all who get to know him.

These two boys showed me the greatest gift God has given me. Motherhood was not what I had imagined it to be. Before Ricardo and I got married, we decided that we did not want children right away. We were very young when we got married. I was just twenty-two, and he was twenty-three. I hadn't finished my college education. He was still pursuing his career. We wanted to be financially stable, finish school, and be able to travel. My mom always told me, "Get that all out of your system because when you have children, everything changes."

We did everything we had set out to do and were married for ten years before having kids. I finished my bachelor's degree and then got my master's degree. We started our business together. In my human thinking, we did everything right. When we started the family, I had my firstborn son while still trying to run the business. I kept thinking daily, *Really? This is God's grand plan? I went through all this schooling and planning, only to be wiping butts and sucking snot all day.*

In a way, I was resenting motherhood. Society lies to us—to women especially, telling us that we can have it all or that we're supposed to strive to have it all. I'm supposed to be a career woman. I'm supposed to be a lover. I'm supposed to be a mother. I'm supposed to be a Michelin star chef. I'm supposed to work out five times a week and look like I'm twenty years old forever. All while putting on a happy face, loving it and feeling empowered by it. And if I don't, then I have failed as a "strong, powerful, independent woman."

I felt pulled in a million different directions. Because I believed those lies that unless I was in some executive tower executing my MBA, my intelligence, gifts, and talents weren't worth anything. But when the real threat of having my children taken away from me was staring me in the eyes, I couldn't care less about my MBA. I couldn't care less about my business. I couldn't care less about being in a pantsuit in an executive meeting. All I wanted was my children and my family.

God used this nightmare to reveal what role He created for me in my family. A role so much bigger than any executive paycheck or a diploma could offer me. God made me—us! Women—to be life-givers, and the devil hates that. Mothering means laying down one's life for another, which is symbolic of what He did for us. The devil also knows that we will raise little arrows directly aimed at the kingdom of darkness. He knows we play the most important role of anyone. When I understood this, instead of enduring and complaining about the drudgery of everyday life and raising children, I now consider everything an act of worship and obedience to God.

But I still asked, "God, why did I even bother going to college then? What is this?" And God spoke to my heart, *I will use your talents in due time. But for now, look after your sons. Look at those boys. They need you. And this is where I've planted you. This is where I want you. But in due time, I will use your talents.* I will use those expensive pieces of paper on the wall. That's what I call my diplomas—expensive pieces of paper. And I believe it is now "due time."

Seeing my son in that medically induced coma, witnessing fifteen seizures an hour, and the doctors not knowing what cocktail of medication to give to him. Being in those child abuse classes seeing parent, after parent, after parent getting their children taken away. Getting their children adopted. Getting their parental rights terminated. I don't know how I would have survived had I not had women who were like-minded and solid in the Word. I learned how important is it who we surround ourselves with.

My marriage. Had I not had a God-fearing man by my side, I don't think we would have lasted. Throughout our case, the system purposely tried to pit us against each other. Our marriage did not come out of this unscathed. We went through two years of counseling. One of the most well-known Bible verses, Ecclesiastes 4:12—And though a man might prevail against one who is alone, two will withstand him—a threefold cord is not quickly broken—became a living example to us. We were "equally yoked" (2 Corinthians 6:14) and knew that our commitment was not only to each other but to God himself. Love without commitment is not love.

"You're enough." Just take one scroll down your social media timeline, and you'll see this quote. When it came to a moment like this, when my whole world was pulled out from underneath me, I realized, *I am not enough. I am nothing. I am nothing without God.* And yes, God will use me because He made me capable of such things. But I must obey if I want to see His plans come to fruition in my life.

During our case, I searched for the truth and focused on what had happened to Lucas. I prayed daily: *May the truth be revealed.* But God showed me another truth. In the child abuse classes, parenting classes, and individual counseling, God revealed the truth to me was about this system. I would never have believed it had it not happened to me.

Having grown up in church, I had always heard about foster care and adoption being beautiful things. People would frequently take Bible verses about "helping the widow and the orphan" or about us "being adopted into God's family." Therefore, adopting a child is sort of equivalent to what God did for us. Except there's a problem. Most of these children were *not* orphans. They had another parent, they had grandparents, they had aunts and uncles—what they didn't have was money. Knowing what I know today, I can never look at adoption the same way again. The money that was offered to my mom at the time, $680 a month per child, comes from the Federal Government. The States get anywhere from $2-$6K a month for every child that is placed in Foster Care. The system has no incentive for reunification, even though that language is in their policies. The truth is kinship placement (family members) get less money from the state than placement with "certified foster families" (strangers). This seems very backwards if you ask me.

During my interaction with my fellow CAT parents, they became my friends ... or more like brothers. As the Bible says in Proverbs 17:17, "A friend loves at all times, and a brother is born for adversity." Most of them were in unfortunate circumstances financially. Yes, some made bad decisions in their relationships, but no one had intentionally abused their children. I cannot imagine living not knowing where my children are, not even being able to tell them my side of the story. Unfortunately, that's what happens when this government entity takes over what is rightfully the parent's role.

God gave me an unbelievable love for these families. An indescribable love for mothers that can only come from Him. Listening to their stories, nobody had abused their children. There were accidents. There were even incidences of domestic violence where the children would end up going to the abuser. Nothing made sense.

During that prayer, where I asked God who should repent, I prayed, "What did I do? What did I do to deserve this?" And the Holy Spirit whispered in my heart that it was just the evil world, the fallen world we live in.

The revelation of truth was that this system is not being used to protect children. It's not being used to help families. It's being used to destroy families, which is what Satan has been doing from the beginning of time—destroy the family. It changed my perspective about everything. Writing a book about this story would never have been my choice, but it has now become my calling.

I was essentially raised by a single mother. My father passed away when I was nine months old. My mom came to this country without speaking a word of English, with nothing but a suitcase in hand. My mom was going to school and sometimes working two to three jobs at a time to support me. At times I stayed home alone. I would make myself a sandwich or whatever was left over from dinner.

As a teenager, I got in some gnarly fights with my mom. I remember one day I ditched school, and it was raining. My mom innocently took an umbrella to the school office so I wouldn't have to walk home in the rain, only to find out that I had not come to school that day. The police were called, and they went searching for me. I remember stepping out of the McDonalds, and a police officer called me over and said, "I'm looking for someone that fits your description. What's your name?"

I answered, "Rachel."

He said, "Yep, that's you. Get in here," gesturing me to get in the car.

I remember freaking out and asking him, "What did I do wrong?!"

He chuckled and asked, "Why are you skipping school?"

"Because I hate it there," I responded.

He then asked me what my relationship was like with my mom, where my dad was, if my mom had any boyfriends … a line of questioning sounding eerily familiar to me now. All my responses could have been misconstrued or twisted to remove me from my home. It would have destroyed me to have been taken away from my mom, my only blood relative in the US. The only one who I could talk to about my dad, our families in Brazil, my culture, and where I came from. Yet I could have been removed because of alleged "neglect" or "failure to protect" if a neighbor had called because I had run away or because they heard my mom and me fighting. Thankfully, even back then, God always had His veil of protection over me.

My mom and I did not have any government assistance, but we did have community. We had a church family. When my mom had to go to work or had an appointment, I stayed at their house. If we had to go to another part of town where we couldn't take the bus, somebody would drive us over there. That's what it means to take care of the widow and the orphan—help these families by bringing them a home-cooked meal, offer to watch the kids after school. Or, if it's beyond your skill level and they need psychological help or rehab, contact a non-profit organization or your local church.

The Christian community has been blinded by this idea of intervening as a form of helping, as if calling the authorities is a form of helping. But the Bible itself tells us that if you have a problem with your brother or your neighbor, contact a mediator or try to take care of it among yourselves before calling law enforcement or a third party. That is very wise advice because once you get the government or the authorities involved, chances are this child, this mother, this father, will never be reunited again. If they are reunited, they will be monitored constantly and traumatized for the rest of their lives.

Poverty can look a lot like neglect if a child has holes in their shoes or their clothes. If a child looks unkempt, or if they've been eating nothing but chicken nuggets all week. If there's a pile of dirty dishes in the sink. Whatever the case may be, depending on what social worker shows up at your door, they can spin it to fit the government's definition of neglect or abuse.

When these familial bonds are destroyed without necessity, we create broken humans who then grow up to become dependent on other vices, creating a vicious cycle. A cycle of abuse, dependency, and brokenness. As much intervention as a society may want to offer psychologically, financially, and socially, I know that the healer of broken hearts is God through Jesus. He's what these families need and what these children need.

I hope someday to create a non-profit organization, a one-stop shop where I can house these moms going through a "child abuse" investigation and dealing with having their children removed. A monitored facility so that these moms do not lose their children; a place where psychological services, rehabilitation services, and legal services may be offered without judgment or coercion.

And at the center of it all, a prayer team—a movement of prayer against the destruction of the family. We went through was a spiritual battle, which had to be fought with spiritual weapons. Prayer is an essential weapon to have in one's arsenal.

To this day, I have met hundreds of families enduring the same ordeal. I always tell them the outcome of my case was only possible by the grace of God. I am not a better parent than them. I am not a better person because I am educated, nor am I more deserving of our outcome. I step out into this crazy world of advocacy as a servant to God's calling. I want nothing more than to reach the gates of Heaven and hear: "Well done good and faithful servant" (Matthew 25:23). God created the family. There's nothing more precious in this life.

Extra Offers

Complimentary Devotional

Download the accompanying study guide by going to:
  www.rachelbruno.com/fracturedhope

Review

Your opinions are important and I truly value your feedback. As an author it is important to get **Reviews** from valuable readers like you so that future readers can make better decisions. Please help me by leaving your honest review on your preferred bookstore or platform. Thank you!

Share

If you enjoyed this book and found the content useful, please share it with your friends online. Use the hashtag #FracturedHope and tag me @rachelbrunospeaks so I can thank you:)

Connect with Rachel Online

Facebook https://www.facebook.com/rachelbrunospeaks
Instagram https://www.instagram.com/rachelbrunospeaks

Author Bio

Rachel Bruno is a wife to her husband of 18 years and a mom of two boys. She has a master's degree in Business Administration and co-founded a successful Cyber Security company in 2010 with her husband.

As a business and communication specialist, her goals were to start a business and become financially independent so she could start a family. Things drastically changed in the summer of 2015, shortly after her second child was born.

Rachel's faith carried her through the unimaginable. Her seven-week-old baby and toddler son were seized by Child Protective Services when her newborn was critically injured while a nanny watched him. She was evicted from her own home and faced jail time for a crime she did not commit. The Court put her sons through a battery of invasive medical tests without the Bruno's consent. She fought back and took the government agencies to court. She won her legal case in 2018 and was awarded seven figures in damages.

Rachel is now an author and public speaker. Her focus is to educate families while being a voice for those who have been victimized by the unconstitutional vices of Family Court and Child Protective Services. Through the pain of her experience, she realized her calling: to fearlessly proclaim the role of women in the family and the gift that comes with it.

To learn more about Rachel please visit www.rachelbruno.com

Notes

Notes

www.ingramcontent.com/pod-product-compliance
Ingram Content Group UK Ltd.
Pitfield, Milton Keynes, MK11 3LW, UK
UKHW051450110425
5438UKWH00034B/381